Melrose, Florida:
An Illustrated History

by

Rosemary Daurer
Kevin McCarthy

2017

ISBN-13: 978-1542430791   ISBN-10: 1542430798

Acknowledgments

Among the people we wish to thank in the writing of this book are Mary and Mark Barrow; Keith Bollum and Historic Melrose, Inc. and its many volunteers who have made Melrose such a beautiful town over the years; Jean Marshall; the Clay County Archives; Kevin McCarthy's wife, Karelisa Hartigan; University of Florida librarian Peter McKay; the staff of the Interlibrary Loan Office of the Alachua County Public Library, Gainesville, Florida; Keith McInnis, who took a photograph of the painting on the cover of the book.

The illustration on the cover is of the "Alert" boat on Melrose Bay at a time when steamboats connected Melrose and Waldo. The original, a painting by the late Justin Pearson, is located at the Matheson History Museum, which has given us permission to use the image.

Dedication

We dedicate this history to all the residents, past and present, who have lived in Melrose, especially those who have made great contrbutions to the town, for example Joe and Rosemary Daurer, who amassed an immense collection of the town's photographs, many of which we used in this book.

Corrections

If anyone has corrections for future editions, please email them to Kevin McCarthy: ceyhankevin@gmail.com

CONTENTS

Introduction   1

Chapter One: Location and Geography   3
Chapter Two: The First Inhabitants in the Area   5
Chapter Three: 16th - 19th Century   9
      1820s - 10   1840s - 12   1850s - 14   1860s - 15
      1870s - 18   1880s - 39   1890s - 55
Chapter Four: 20th Century   74
      1900s - 74   1910s - 94   1920s - 105   1930s - 111
      1940s - 118   1950s - 125   1960s - 128   1970s - 129
      1980s - 146   1990s - 154
Chapter Five: 21st Century   158
      2000s - 158   2010s - 169
Conclusion   170
Appendix 1 - Civil War Veterans   172
Appendix 2 - World War I Veterans   173
Appendix 3 - World War II Veterans   173

Scenes around Melrose in 2017   176
About the authors   180
Bibliography   181
Photo credits   183

Index   184

Scenes of Melrose Today

Melrose Bay

Melrose Bay Park

INTRODUCTION

Melrose is on the southeastern shore of Santa Fe Lake. The town's relatively high elevation (about 145 feet above sea level) makes it a healthy place to live because it is above the low swamps elsewhere.

Roughly forty percent of the town lies in Alachua County, forty percent in Putnam County, ten percent in Bradford County, and ten percent in Clay County. It may, in fact, be the only town in America that is in four counties.

The town is 20 miles east of Gainesville, 25 miles west of Palatka, and 65 miles southwest of Jacksonville. It has no industries or large businesses, but instead has farms that raise blueberries and oranges, vineyards for grapes made into wine and jellies, and nurseries for landscape plants. Occasional freezes hurt the local crops, but in general the climate is very mild.

Melrose Bay

Today the town is no longer incorporated. Therefore one can only guess at the number of residents, some of whom are only part-time, living in weekend or holiday residences along the lake. Some eighteen thousand people live within a five-mile radius of the town.

The town has a very large green space (Heritage Park) in the center of town, a park with a playground for children, a history museum, a veterans' memorial, even a gazebo for musical performers.

Heritage Park

The town has a number of churches, as well as several very fine restaurants, art galleries, two gas stations, a library, and a few businesses, but there is no movie theater or nightclub. If residents want those, they can make the relatively easy drive to Gainesville or Palatka, and, in fact, some residents commute to those towns for work.

Chapter One: Location and Geography

Much of the appeal of Melrose over the past two hundred years is no doubt its proximity to these bodies of water: Lake Alto, Santa Fe Lake, Little Santa Fe Lake, and Melrose Bay. Those are spring-fed and rain-fed, but receive most of their water from the Santa Fe Swamp, a floodplain swamp which feeds into and supplies water to the Santa Fe River, which drains into the Suwannee River and eventually the Gulf of Mexico.

The Florida Fish and Wildlife Conservation Commission (FWC) acquired the Santa Fe Swamp, which it manages today in cooperation with the Suwannee River Water Management District (SRWMD). Most of the 7,272 acres in the Santa Fe Swamp Wildlife and Environmental Area (WEA) are dense swamps. The swamp lies just north of Little Santa Fe Lake.

The aerial photo to the right shows Little Santa Fe Lake at the top, then Santa Fe Lake below that, and Melrose Bay at the lower right.

Santa Fe Lake (or Lake Santa Fe) is a 5,850-acre spring-fed lake in northeastern Alachua County bounded on the east and south sides by Bradford County, Clay County, and Putnam County. The lake, one of the largest and most stable in the state, offers excellent fishing and recreational boating, as well as opportunities to see a wide variety of wildlife. It is followed in size by Little Lake Santa Fe and Melrose Bay, as well as Lake Alto further away.

Santa Fe Lake, which receives much of its water from springs, has an average depth of about 19.5 feet and a maximum depth of about 25 feet. Little Santa Fe Lake has a surface area of 1425 acres, but is relatively shallow, having an average depth of about fourteen feet and a maximum depth of 23 feet. It is connected to Santa Fe Lake by a short waterway called "The Pass." Little Lake Santa Fe is connected to Lake Alto by a shallow canal built in 1881 for steamboats (more details in the section on the 1870s). Melrose Bay has a surface area of about 52 acres, an average depth of fifteen feet, and a maximum depth of 23 feet.

This was a color photograph from the late 1800s entitled "On the banks of the Santa Fe."

Chapter Two: The First Inhabitants in the Area

Around 50,000 years ago, much of the earth's waters was frozen in glaciers, and the level of the oceans was as much as 350 feet lower than today. The North American continent. in fact, was joined to Asia at the Bering Strait west of where Alaska is today.

Asian hunters made their way across the land bridge, which scientists call Beringia, to look for animals like the giant mastodon and mammoth. The hunters spread out over all of North America and settled down with their families in places where they could hunt and fish.

Large mammoths like these used to roam through Florida, as indicated by their bones and fossils found in phosphate pits and deep springs, for example Wakulla Springs near Tallahassee.

About 12,000 years ago, some of those people reached Florida. Archaeologists call those first Floridians Paleoindians. Those first Americans chose to live in places where they could hunt, fish, raise crops, and support their families.

North-central Florida offered many suitable places for the new settlers to flourish. The area had forests full of plants and animals; rivers and lakes that had fish and turtles; proximity to the ocean with its vast numbers of fish, turtles, and shellfish; and the ability to travel to offshore islands in large canoes.

When **Juan Ponce de León** and his followers arrived on the Atlantic coast of northeast Florida in 1513 in the Easter season, the Florida peninsula had at least 250,000 Indians, who were grouped into some one hundred different tribes.

According to archaeologists like **Jerald Milanich**, one of the major Indian tribes in north Florida in the sixteenth and seventeenth centuries, for example along the St. Johns, was the Timucua. Other groups were the Apalachee in the northwestern part of the peninsula and the Calusa in the southwest.

Above is an engraving by **Theodorus de Bry** *(1528 – 1598), who never came to America, but who primarily based his images on the descriptions of an artist,* **Jacques Le Moyne**, *who did come here with* **René Laudonnière** *in 1564; this picture shows Timucua Indians having a conference.*

A major clue to the presence of Native Americans in Florida is the shell mound, also known as a tumulus, platform mound, burial mound, and midden. While there used to be thousands of such mounds in Florida, road-builders have leveled many of them and used the compacted shell remnants for the roads.

Or developers leveled the mounds, before such practice was forbidden by law, to build in their places luxurious houses.

The Native-American mound at Crystal River State Archaeological Site

Major middens/shell mounds in North Florida may be seen at Mount Royal along the St. Johns River several miles south of Palatka and north of Drayton Island on the east shore of the river. On the west coast of Florida on Crystal River one can visit a major midden/shell mound of the pre-Columbian Native Americans.

The 61-acre site has six large mounds that include burial mounds, temple mounds, and a substantial plaza area. Native Americans used the ceremonial center there for some 1,600 years, making it one of the longest continuously occupied sites in Florida.

Searchers have found evidence of the presence of Native Americans in the Melrose area, evidence consisting of mounds and artifacts like arrowheads and pottery. The photo below shows **Leigh Pearsall** excavating a nearby Indian mound with a friend. Pearsall's collection is now housed at the new Florida Museum of Natural History on the campus of the University of Florida in Gainesville.

Leigh Pearsall (on right) at Indian Mound in Melrose area —early 1900s

Kennie Howard, in her book about Melrose entitled *Yesterday in Florida,* noted that one large Indian mound was off Orange Springs Road (now S.R. 21) south of Melrose and near the old watermill at Etoniah Creek.

Chapter Three: 16th - 19th Century

Within 150 years of the arrival of the Spaniards in Florida in 1513, the weapons and diseases of the Europeans had killed millions of Native Americans in the New World, including those in the Florida peninsula.

Many Indians also died after the Spaniards took them away from their tribes to carry the supplies that the Spanish army needed. Also, because the Spanish soldiers stole food from the Indians along the way, many Native American tribes faced severe food shortages after the Spanish passed through their territory.

In the 1700s, a group of Native Americans split off from the Lower Creek Indians in present-day South Georgia and headed south to Florida, where most of the Native Americans had died of diseases brought by the Europeans or in the constant warfare among tribes. At that time, only a few thousand white settlers were living in the peninsula, mostly around St. Augustine. The word "Seminole," which was used to describe many of the Native Americans, is a corruption of the Spanish term *cimarrón*, which meant "runaway" or "wild one."

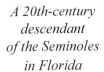

A 20th-century descendant of the Seminoles in Florida

1820s

Two years after Florida became a U.S. Territory (1821), surveyors described the area of Melrose as "an uninhabited wilderness, except (for) a few Indian villages."

Three years later (1824) the U.S. Congress, in an effort to connect the two main cities of Florida (St. Augustine and Pensacola) with the territorial capital (Tallahassee), authorized the building of what came to be called the Bellamy Road – so called after the main builder: **John Bellamy**. The road was to be 25 feet wide, which would allow two wagons to pass each other without stopping.

The building of the road was begun in 1824, the same year that Alachua County was established. The project took two years to finish, but what turned out to be Florida's first federal highway did much to join East and West Florida, as well as make travel inland much easier than before.

In the eastern part of Alachua County, the road went along the south end of Santa Fe Lake in what would become State Road 26 in Melrose.

The Bellamy Road looked much like this across northern Florida.

In the nineteenth century the Seminole Indians fought three major wars with federal troops and with local settlers over who would control Florida.

Under the leadership of great warriors like **Osceola** (pictured to the left), the Indians won some of the battles between 1816 and 1858, but in the end were killed, fled south to the Everglades, or were captured and sent west to the Indian Territory.

Those Seminoles who fled south to the Everglades were not pursued by federal troops. The Native Americans settled down, raised their families, and are, for the most part, thriving today in the state.

H. Von Noszky wrote in an article entitled "An Indian Battlefield near Melrose," in *The Florida Historical Quarterly* (see Bibliography) that Spanish explorer **Hernando de Soto** and his soldiers fought the Native Americans under their chief **Vitachuco** in 1539 near the town, also called Vitachuco after the chief.

The battlefield was near modern-day Two Mile Pond, which is just west of Lake Rosa and south of U.S. 26 to the east of Melrose. Diggers have claimed that they found evidence for the battle in April, 1909.

1840s

After the end of the Second Seminole War in 1842, new settlers came to north-central Florida, urged on by the granting of free land to homesteaders by the federal government. In August, 1842, Congress had passed the Armed Occupation Act, which gave free land to settlers who improved their property and agreed to defend themselves from attacks by Native Americans.

From 1821, when Florida became a territory of the United States, until the mid-nineteenth century transportation here was either by foot, horse, carriage, or boat. Because the St. Johns River flowed north, it became one of the chief means by which settlers could travel up and down the interior of the peninsula on the east coast. Those who wanted to travel toward the Gulf coast and farmers/ranchers who needed to ship their crops/livestock elsewhere eventually looked to the railroad for transportation.

Settlers began to build homesteads like this one
after the end of the Seminole Indian Wars.

In 1845, Florida became a state at the same time that Iowa became one. The former became a slave state, while the latter became a free state, thus balancing power between slave and free states. Florida's entrance into the Union no doubt attracted more and more people to the peninsula.

Florida plantation owners depended on slaves, especially in the growing and harvesting of cotton (see picture to the left). In 1830, Florida had a total population of 34,730, 47% of whom were nonwhite.

In 1840, Florida had a total population of 54,477, 48% of whom were nonwhite. In 1850, the State of Florida had a total population of 87,445, 46% of whom were nonwhite.

The majority of the nonwhite population were slaves; fewer than a thousand of the nonwhite population were free.

Because Florida depended on slave labor to work on its farms and plantations, it became a so-called slave state when it entered the Union.

1850s

After the end of the Seminole Indian Wars in 1842 and before the start of the American Civil War in 1861, white settlers moved into north-central Florida to farm the land and raise their families. The Florida General Assembly passed the Internal Improvement Act of 1855 to encourage residents and developers in the state to build more railroads and canals. That Act would do much to encourage the building of a canal near Waldo.

Florida Senator **David Levy Yulee** built the first railroad across the state from Fernandina in the northeast corner of Florida to Cedar Key on the west coast. Workers completed the line to Gainesville in 1859 and the final stretch to Cedar Key in 1861 with connections in Callahan, Baldwin, Waldo, and Archer. The American Civil War (1861 to 1865), however, put an end to the railroad as troops on both sides of the conflict tore up the rails and rendered it unusable.

The Melrose Cemetery was founded in 1860 and is located .2 mile south of the crossroads on S.R. 21. The Florida historic marker below, erected in 2009, stands at the entrance to the cemetery.

1860s

The American Civil War (1861 – 1865) disrupted life in the area, but after the war Confederate soldiers returned home and new settlers began arriving once again. Reconstruction was hard in many parts of Florida, until federal troops withdrew in 1877. The soldiers and new settlers around the area grew crops, including citrus. Many of those from the North traveled down to Jacksonville by boat and train and then continued on the Bellamy Road to Palatka, Waldo, and other small towns. After the war, newly emancipated slaves, called Freedmen, hired on as workers on local farms or as sharecroppers. Black women began working as wet nurses and maids.

The cemetery organized in 1860 was the Melrose Cemetery, near the Eliam Baptist Church, which began in 1859. The cemetery was also known as the Banana Burying Ground for the nearby community of Banana. The earliest tombstone dates back to 1861, and two hundred of the grave stones have dates earlier than 1900.

Melrose founders and developers are buried there, for example Dr. **Frank McRae** (pictured to the right - the grave site is about 34 yards from the entrance to the cemetery) and directly behind the cemetery sign.

Civil War soldiers from the Melrose area

A stele in Heritage Park off S.R. 26 has a list of 42 men from the Melrose area who served in the Civil War and includes six Union soldiers, who moved to Melrose after the war. See the appendix for a list of the names on the Civil War memorial. The list was compiled by by the co-author of this book, **Rosemary Daurer.**

A memorial to all those who served in the military from the Melrose area stands outside the Melrose Cemetery.

A church in the 1860s

The Eliam Baptist Church in 1860

The first Eliam Baptist Church, pictured here in 1860, was in Banana at the cemetery.

The Eliam Baptist Church on Park and Hampton streets in 2016

1870s
Banana

The area called Banana took its name from the banana plants that grew along Etoniah Creek near the Eliam Baptist Church. Officials established the Banana Post Office on May 20, 1875. The postmaster was Dr. **George Washington Alexander "Wash" McRae**, a general practitioner and the owner of the Banana mill, which he built in 1885 on Etoniah Creek.

Photo from the Daurer Collection
How Old Mill at Banana Looked in the 1930's

Dr. **Frank McRae**, the cousin of Dr. **G.W. McRae**, studied medicine at the University of New York at Albany, where he graduated in 1870, Dr. McRae, according to **Zonira Tolles**, author of two books about Melrose, quoted his obituary, which said he "'did more real charitable work among the poor than any man in this section ... [and] consequently he died a poor man.'"(*Bonnie Melrose*, p. 67)

A model of the mill on Etoniah Creek - the model, which was crafted by **Pat Warren**, *is part of the Historic Melrose Inc. collection in the organization's building.*

The mill that **George "Wash" McRae** built on Etoniah Creek was driven by a twelve-horsepower water turbine that was three feet in diameter. The mill ground up the corn that local farmers brought in, for which services they paid the miller a portion of the corn, usually about fifty per cent.

The machine poured the shelled corn into a hopper, where large, stone disks rotated the corn and ground it into corn meal or flour. The noisy mill could be heard all around the community when the grinding was taking place. The mill continued to operate until the 1930s.

Brian Michaels in his history of Putnam County (see Bibliography) cites a report that Banana had a post office from May 20, 1875 through 1883. One local Melrose resident told us that she thought the mail carrier in the mid-1870s would drop off mail for residents in the area at Dr. McRae's establishment, which apparently doubled as a post office. After the Banana Post Office was discontinued in 1883, the local residents went to Melrose to get their mail. The Melrose post office was established in 1878.

Christopher & Catherine McRae

For more about the McRae Family, see the book to the right (see Bibliography).

The remnants of the mill now under a shed above the creek

The site of Banana is about 1.2 miles south of the traffic light in Melrose on S.R. 21, but it is not open to the public. Historic Melrose, Inc., is in charge of the site and occasionally has tours to the site.

The site of the post office (above) and well (below) are marked at the place.

Dr. George Washington McRae

Dr. **G.W. McRae** was one of the most important early developers of Banana and then Melrose. He first came to the area around 1855 and began acquiring large tracts of land.

In 1859, he joined Eliam Baptist Church and sold the parishioners property to build a cemetery and the first Baptist church building on present-day S.R. 21. He was a medical doctor, farmer, owner of a general store, postmaster, and operator of a grist mill in Banana.

Dr. G.W.A. Mc Rae of Melrose, FL about 1895. Picture published in the 7 Nov 1895 Atlanta Journal/Constitution newspaper

He became a school trustee and helped organize the Etoniah Stream Dredge and Canal Company. He also served as an officer in the Civil War. The picture here is one of the few images that we have of Dr. McRae.

Bonnie Mount, one of the first buildings in the area

When Melrose was surveyed and platted in 1877, two brothers from Kentucky, **William** and **C.D. Bonney**, were already living in a farmhouse, called the Bonney Farm, on Melrose Bay: 741 Seminole Ridge Road today, directly across the Bay from Bayview. It was later called "Bonney Place," "Bonnie View," and "Bonnie Mount."

Bonnie Mount in its early days

The two brothers, one of whom had a wife and baby, farmed vegetables on about one hundred acres on the north side of Melrose Bay. Their old barn is across the road on private property.

Bonnie Mount today

When the Bonneys later moved back to Kentucky, the Lambdins, who had built Bayview across Melrose Bay, acquired the Bonney land and moved there when Mr. Lambdin lost Bay-view.

In the mid-1870s, in the decade after the end of the Civil War, the Florida Railroad had new rails laid down and was ready for business. As **Caroline Watkins** described in her article entitled "Some Early Railroads in Alachua County": "A reorganization was ordered, and with new capital two locomotives were purchased and extensive improvements were begun. The name of the road was changed to the Atlantic, Gulf and West India Transit Company. Four years later a connecting line was extended from Waldo to Ocala." (p. 451).

The train left Fernandina each day for Gainesville and three times weekly for Cedar Key. Transporting the produce by wagon to the railroad depot, for example at Waldo, was still difficult since the sandy roads were difficult to manage, especially during the rainy season. The photo below shows the Waldo train depot, which was built in 1864. Many agreed that a canal would make transporting goods to the train much easier than by wagon.

Seaboard Depot, Waldo, Fla.

Carl Webber's *Eden of the South* (1883) described what he called the "lake region" in the eastern half of Alachua County, including Melrose and Banana:

> "[the area] is far away from the bleak, damp atmosphere of the coast, and free from the malarial and miasmatic diseases in the section of the State, and, all seasons together, it is as healthy as any spot on the continent where people can live and make a living. The land through all this section is high, slightly rolling, with pine, oak and hickory growth interspersed. Where the land is not rich enough for vegetable products, it is excellent for oranges and other fruits, and thus it is interspersed as if made to order." (p. 32)

Interestingly, Webber in that 1883 work thought that Melrose was an "outgrowth of Banana," but the former would soon overshadow the latter town. Those living in small towns like Melrose wondered if they could reach Waldo by water, an efficient and relatively cheaper means of transportation than other means. Could they reach Waldo eleven miles away by using the lakes and maybe a canal between the two lakes?

Remnants of the Santa Fe Canal today, as seen from Highway 1471

Officials chartered the Santa Fe Canal Company on March 2, 1877. Surveyor **Ned Farrell** was the one who did the survey to see if a canal was feasible from Santa Fe Lake and Lake Alto to Waldo. Workers began building a canal between the lakes and finished the work in 1881. The completed canal was some five feet deep and thirty feet wide.

The dredging of the canal to Waldo -
This drawing is from "Eden of the South," 1883.

The canal allowed passengers to go by railroad from Jacksonville to Waldo and then by steamer on Lake Alto to Melrose. The powerful dredge that dug the canal was a steam-powered, wood-burning vessel, but keeping the canal free of hyacinths and sand that was washed in from the sides would become a never-ending task. Workers would load goods along Santa Fe Lake, take them to Lake Alto, load them onto a spur of the railroad, and take them to Waldo and the Fernandina – Cedar Key Railroad.

A sketch of the F.S. Lewis

The first steamboat to take people and freight on the canal was the *F.S. Lewis,* which made her inaugural trip through the canal to Santa Fe Lake on April 26, 1881, and after that made the trip through the lakes to Waldo twice a day. In Waldo passengers could connect with the railroad that went across the state from Fernandina to Cedar Key.

Carl Webber's *Eden of the South*, from which the above drawing of the *F.S. Lewis* was taken, described the boat as being nearly one hundred feet long and twenty feet wide. It had room for two hundred passengers.

The boat allowed farmers access to markets elsewhere. Webber described the Melrose area as "one of the most healthy and desirable sections, among rolling hills and hundreds of beautiful clear water lakes." (p.22)

When the steamboat was operating and keeping to its schedule, people would gather each morning at 8:30 a.m. to see the vessel head off and then again at 4:30 p.m. to see her return.

The steamboat *F.S. Lewis*, which may have been named after a local cotton farmer and may have been built in Waldo by those who knew the nearby lakes and the new canal, was plagued by difficulties like a broken drive-shaft soon after it entered service.

Worse than that was the fact that the large size of the vessel prevented it from stopping at the smaller landings, for example Earleton. On one trip, the boat capsized during a storm, had to be righted, but then caught fire and sank on Santa Fe Lake around 1884.

The Alert *was smaller than the* F.S.Lewis, *but often towed a barge behind it for more storage space for cargo, including fertilizer for the new orange groves in the area.*

The second boat landing in Melrose

To solve the problems of the bulky *F.S. Lewis*, developers replaced it with a smaller vessel called *Alert*, which they bought in Jacksonville and took to Alachua County by flatcar. The *Alert* was able to transport passengers and freight through the Waldo Canal and across the lakes. The steamboats sometimes towed a little rowboat behind so that if the big boat broke down, someone could get in the small boat and row to shore.

The first boat landing was where Bayview was located (see p. 37) when **McKendrie Lambdin** worked with the canal company. It was he who built Bayview overlooking Melrose Bay. Then after a short time workers moved the dock or built a new one a block east – at Trout Street.

The dock and building are gone, but the county operates a boat-launching place where the second dock was. There are no photos of the first dock/landing, but the old photo above shows the second one.

Another photo of the Alert *with passengers*

Three early residents who saw the potential of Melrose on the south side of Santa Fe Lake, **Alexander Goodson**, **Meredith Granger**, and **Isaac Weston**, hired **William L. Sims** to lay out a plan for the town.

Officials recorded the plat in the courthouses of Alachua, Bradford, Clay, and Putnam counties on May 10, 1877, a date considered the official founding date of the town.

Ned Farrell, the man who had surveyed the canal to Waldo, also bought some land on the shore of a lake northeast of Melrose, surveyed it, and platted a town site there that he called Geneva. He also changed the name of the lake from "No 11" to "Lake Geneva."

A freight boat in the canal

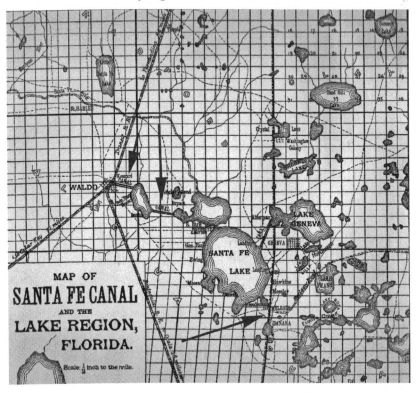

An early map of the area showing an arrow pointing to Melrose/Banana and two arrows pointing to canals from the lakes toward Waldo

Pictures of "The Alert"

The steamboat at a wharf in Melrose

*The boat at a dock on Trout Street in Melrose -
see also the image on the cover of this book.*

Keeping the canal free of hyacinths was a difficult job, and soon the invasive plants clogged it, as seen in this photo of another Florida canal.

Four scenes of the canal when it was free of hyacinths.

The canal served a very important role in transporting goods and people to and from Melrose and Waldo, but the coming of automobiles, trucks, and trains ended its usefulness in the first quarter of the twentieth century.

The era of the steamboats lasted from 1881 to the 1920s. At that time other means of transportation (cars, buses, trucks, trains, eventually planes) superseded the steamboats and provided faster, more reliable, safer transport, especially as the road system of the United States improved each decade.

According to *Florida Place Names* by **Allen Morris**, the original name of the area north of present-day Melrose, Shakerag, derived from the way that pony races were started on Sundays on the dirt track there: the starter would shake a large white cloth or rag instead of wasting a bullet to start the race.

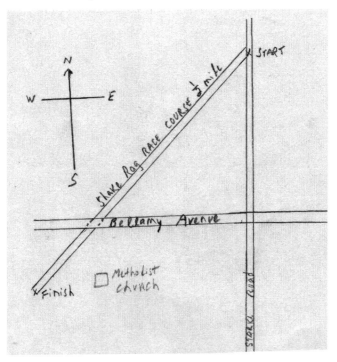

This hand-drawn map, based on the best available sources for the 1870s, shows the half-mile racetrack that ended where the Methodist Church is today.

The races may have been held on what was called the Lewis Plantation. There does not seem to have been any settlement near the pony racetrack.

The races ended just west of where the United Methodist Church is today. That church, pictured as it looked in 2016, is the oldest church building in Melrose, having been built around 1879. The bell tower used to be more elaborate. Its bell was used for several purposes, including the announcement of a fire or a death in the community.

The interior of the church in December, 2016

The McKendrie Lambdin Family

One of the most important early developers of what became Melrose was **McKendrie Lambdin.** In her book, *Yesterday in Florida*, Mrs. **Kennie Lambdin Howard** wrote how her father, McKendrie Lambdin, came from a prominent Virginia family who supported the American Revolution and whose men fought in the war.

McKendrie fought in the Civil War and was seriously wounded in 1865. After the war he became a Mississippi River steamboat worker. He came to Florida when **Robert Ewing**, a former neighbor in Mississippi, encouraged him to move to the Waldo area because of the canal that was being planned there. In 1877, McKendrie Lambdin came to Melrose with his family from Yazoo City, Mississippi. In Florida he became the representative for the Canal Transportation Company for the south end of Santa Fe Lake.

The original Lee House in 1879
*(more about the **Lee Family** in subsequent chapters)*

In 1878, he bought some land in Melrose, property that began at the Bellamy Road and went along the west side of Quail Street to Melrose Bay. He also bought a sawmill, had it moved to the foot of Trout Street, and cut the lumber for Bayview, one of the first houses built in Melrose, next to the steamboat landing. He called it Bayview since it overlooked the beautiful Melrose Bay. It was the only such "hotel-like facility" until the Melrose Inn opened in 1890. Trout Street, by the way, was named, not for a fish caught in the Bay, but for a **Robert Trout**, who owned a business on the street.

Bayview was one of the most elegant buildings in Melrose for many years. The owners of Bayview, the **Lambdins** *(***Ella*** and* **Mac***), used their long living room, called "the Hall," for many town benefits, parties, and musicals.*

37

Kennie Howard in her *Yesterday in Florida* book (p. 67) wrote that the second family to buy land in the area and build a home was Mr. and Mrs. **Greenberry Jackson** and their children. The family came from Ohio and built the first house in the newly platted town of Melrose.

Jackson's son married the granddaughter of **Alex Goodson**, the founder of Melrose. Greenberry's grandson, **Harry Jackson II**, lives in the house on Trout Street at Park Avenue and taught in the Melrose School. Greenberry built a blacksmith shop on their property that faced Park Avenue. It was a common sight to see horses hitched to poles outside the shop, waiting to be shod. His son, Harry Jackson, was an undertaker in the town and sold caskets and had facilities for water and power and even ice.

The Jackson House today

Postmasters

The Melrose postmasters and their dates in office for the 1870s were **M.C. Goodson** (Jan. 3, 1878 – Nov. 7, 1879) and **William T. Craig** (Nov. 7, 1879 – Nov. 15, 1880).

1880s

Residents debate the origin of the name Melrose for the new settlement. According to **Virginia Perkins** in "Melrose: The Bonnie Town by the Bay," a Captain **J.J. Moseley** suggested the name of Melrose in honor of Melrose, Scotland, where the Melrose Abbey is located.

Captain Moseley, a Confederate soldier and admirer of novelist Sir **Walter Scott,** liked Scotland and, in fact, named a pond on his land Loch Katrina. Moseley was the nephew of **William D. Moseley**, the first governor after Florida became a state in 1845; he served from 1845 until 1849.

Melrose Abbey in Melrose, Scotland

The black arrow in the map to the right points to Melrose in the southeastern part of Scotland.

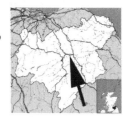

One of the new families to arrive in Melrose around the 1870s -1880s was the **Wolfe Family** from Philadelphia, Pennsylvania: **Mr.** and **Mrs. John Wolfe**, daughter **Emily**, and son **Lynol**. According to **Kennie Howard** in her *Yesterday in Florida* book (p.73) the family built a two-story house in town, and Mr. Wolfe planted an orange grove outside the town.

John Wolfe said that he first became interested in Melrose after reading an article by **Mac Lambdin** and then writing to Mr. Lambdin for more information. The daughter, Emily Wolfe, became a teacher in the town school a few years after the family arrived in Melrose. The Wolfes moved back north after the freezes.

The Wolfe House in Melrose - it is no longer there.

Scenes from the 1880s in Melrose

Some well-dressed citizens gather to paint a fence on Quail Street.

*The citizens painted the fence with Bayview in the background.
According to* **Kennie Howard** *in her* Yesterday in Florida *book, her
parents, the Lambdins, who were the first owners of Bayview, used
pipes laid deep in the ground to take water from the lake to a tank near
the kitchen. They obtained their drinking and cooking water
from a drilled well. (p. 128)*

Churches in Melrose in the 1880s

The church pictured to the right was originally the Methodist Episcopal Church in the early 1880s. It is the oldest church building in Melrose.

The church building pictured here was built around 1879. At one time the bell tower was more elaborate. Its bell was used to announce to the community a fire, death, freeze, or arrival of the boat. Note the stained glass, which you can see from the outside. The church is located at Pearl and Hampton Streets.

METHODIST EPISCOPAL CHURCH, SOUTH MELROSE, FLORIDA.

T.J. Phillips was the pastor when the first parsonage was built in the early 1880s.

ELIAM BAPTIST CHURCH MELROSE FLORIDA — 1883

Pictured above is the second Eliam Baptist Church, which was built in 1883 in the cemetery. It would be replaced by the third Eliam Baptist Church in 1926 at Park and Hampton streets in town.

In the 1880s more settlers arrived and built beautiful homes along Quail Street and around the bay. Many settlers used pine cut at the sawmill in town. When the hard freezes hit the area in 1895 and 1896, many people sold their orange groves and left to find warmer sites further south or moved back north.

Some of the settlers' descendants lived in the beautiful homes, many of which have been restored in recent times.

Melrose School, part one

The original Melrose School, which was built in 1882, as seen in 1912

Of the four counties that Melrose was located in (Alachua, Bradford, Clay, and Putnam), it was Alachua that supervised the local school and supplied the teachers, even though technically the school was not located in that county. One of the teachers from Gainesville who taught the first classes in the frame building around 1883 – 1884 was a **Mr. Bailey**, assisted by a **Mr. Scott**. Bailey would later be replaced by **Professor Looney**, who would begin a military school in the former Melrose Inn.

The school, located at that time in Clay County where Pine Street and S.R. 21 cross today, was later torn down in 1927. The lumber from the building was used to build the present school gymnasium at the elementary school. In the photo the teacher, **Miss Oberry**, is at the far right in the first row. The present school has one of the four historical markers in Melrose.

Post Office

The first post office (1878 - 1909) in Melrose was on the
corner of Bellamy Road and Hampton Street.
The first post office opened in Melrose in 1878.

Postmasters

The Melrose postmasters and their dates in office for the 1880s were **William T. Craig** (Nov. 7, 1879 – Nov. 15, 1880), **James W. Barnett** (Nov. 15, 1880 – June 19, 1889), **A.P. Painter** (June 19, 1889 – July 24, 1889), and **Lucy M. Fox** (July 24, 1889 – May 8, 1893).

The interior of Trinity Episcopal Church in 2016

Edson Judd completed building the above-pictured Carpenter Gothic-style church in the summer of 1886 at cost of $327.71.

Workers later added a chancel, the part of the inside near the altar that was reserved for the clergy and choir and usually separated from the nave by steps or a screen, in 1895, and stained-glass windows were set in place eleven years later.

Businesses in Melrose in the 1880s

The Husband Brothers had a general merchandise store that decade, but it later burned down. Orville Husband had a general store and post office from 1909 to 1931.

By 1886, the town of Melrose was doing well. It had several general stores, a sawmill, a cotton gin, a livery stable, a meat market, homes, boarding houses, a new high school that cost about $10,000 to build, several churches, a pharmacy, and various shops that served the community, for example a barber, smith, wagon-repair shop, and a blacksmith.

Kennie Howard in her *Yesterday in Florida* book wrote that the town had over five hundred people living in town in the 1880s and almost as many outside or near the town with children attending the Melrose School. (p. 86)

One of the industries in Melrose in the last part of the 19th
century was a cotton gin, pictured above.
It provided a good number of jobs for local men.

Another local industry, at least until the devastating freezes
in 1894 – 1895, was that of packing oranges
for shipment to the North.

The Charleston Earthquake of 1886

1886 saw something happen in Florida, including Melrose, that was very rare: an earthquake. The so-called "Charleston Earthquake of 1886," which occurred on August 31 of that year at a magnitude of 7.0, caused fifty deaths and damage estimated at between $5 million and $6 million to two thousand buildings in the Southeast.

The arrow points to Charleston, South Carolina, the epicenter of an earthquake in 1886 that was felt in Melrose.

Paul Pinckney, writing twenty years later in the *San Francisco Chronicle*, noted that "… the rumors current on the outside were to the effect that Charleston and all the coast country had been swept away by a mighty tidal wave and that the Florida peninsula had snapped off from the continent in the general cataclysm and fallen into the sea."

Kennie Howard wrote in her *Yesterday in Florida* book that "Doors rattled [in Melrose], windows shook, the floor moved slightly under them, prisms above the table tinkled. The chandelier swayed, moved back and forth gently." (p. 142) Other than a few rattled nerves, Melrose did not really suffer from the quake, but it did make residents of the state realize that it could experience a rare earthquake.

Closing Date of School

One expected problem with the fact that Melrose was located in four counties (Alachua, Bradford, Clay, and Putnam) concerned the closing date of the school year.

The question dealt with when children from the different counties would drop out of school on their county's closing day. Although the schoolchildren all registered as having Melrose addresses, they would leave school at the end of the school year, depending on when their home counties determined the last day of school.

According to **Kennie Howard** in her *Yesterday in Florida* book, the situation "resulted in confusion and uncertainty as to who would be attending the final school days in Springtime." (p. 143) For example, all of those in the last grade would rehearse for commencement exercises, but would fail to tell their teachers that they would be leaving school before the actual commencement.

At a special meeting in Melrose of concerned parents, two men, **Mac Lambdin** and **Major Vogelbach**, were elected to go to Tallahassee to try to arrange for all the children to finish the school year on the same date.

The two emissaries succeeded in having the closing date set by Alachua County officials, who supplied most of the teachers. When the townspeople heard the news, a committee of happy residents met the boat carrying Lambdin and Vogelbach when it arrived back in Melrose, as in the photo below.

Local Newspaper

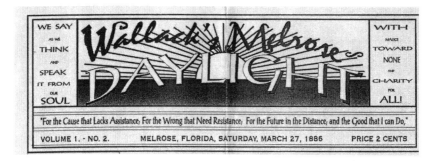

Melrose had a relatively short-lived newspaper in the 1880s called "Wallach's Melrose Daylight," a semi-monthly publication.
The image above was produced by Historic Melrose, Inc., from a very poor copy in the University of Florida Archives.
It shows the first page of vol. 1, no. 2, from March 27, 1886.

Local Inventor

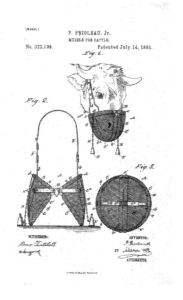

One resident of Melrose, **Philip Priolrau, Jr.,** in 1885 patented a cattle muzzle, which enabled the animal to eat grass and short weeds "with perfect ease and convenience." The muzzle (see picture to the left) prevented the animal from injuring fruit trees while it was pasturing in orchards and orange groves. For a further, detailed description of the muzzle refer to the following internet site: https://www.google.com/patents/US322199.

51

Some of the early houses in Melrose have survived the ravages of time and been carefully restored and preserved.

Dowing W. Sexton, a sea captain from Chatham, Connecticut, had this house built in Melrose on Quail Street in the early 1890s. One of the few so-called "Octagan-style" houses in Florida, this one, nicknamed "Nutmeg," has the shape of the bow of a ship, reflecting Captain Sexton's background.

In 1912, Alfred Pearsall purchased this house on Melrose Bay, restored it, and called it "The Latchstring."

An ad in the local newspaper

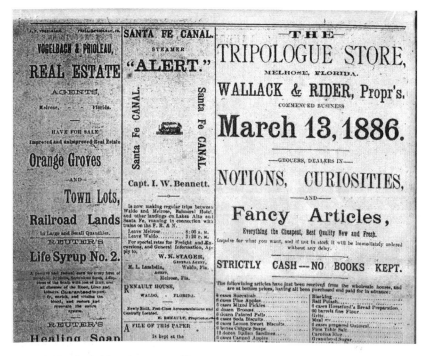

The local businesses offer a variety of goods and services

Melrose School, part one

In 1882, Melrose High School began as a wooden building on Wynwood Street to educate students in west Putnam County and surrounding communities.

This information comes from the historic marker outside the school today. That plaque is one of four in Melrose near significantly historical sites.

1890s

The beginning of the 1890s decade was promising for Melrose: it had connections to towns and markets elsewhere through the railroad and steamboats; more and more people were visiting the town or moving there to settle down; and the town seemed poised to attract even more people to its beautiful lake, surrounding countryside, and rich agricultural fields.

In January, 1890, workers completed building the Green Cove Springs and Melrose Railroad to link Melrose with Green Cove Springs and the Tampa – Jacksonville Railroad, which enabled winter visitors to come to the north-central Florida town. To accommodate the expected influx of visitors, workers built the Santa Fe Hotel in Melrose that same year.

The railroad depot in Melrose on Grove Street (near Pine Street) served the Western Railroad from Green Cove Springs in 1890. Workers later moved it to S.R. 26 and Hampton Street in the early 1900s, where it served as a city hall and public building until it burned down. The railroad line was abandoned after the hard freezes of the mid-1890s.

In 1893, the Lambdins sold Bayview to the Reverend **A.H. Waters**, a Lutheran minister from Jumonville, Pennsylvania, who came to Melrose around 1889. In the early 1890s, he held services in the Mission Chapel.

Soon after buying Bayview, Waters made plans to use the southeast corner of the property at the intersection of Quail and Pine Streets as a lot for St. Luke's Lutheran Church, which workers built in 1894. Rev. Waters was an important member of the community and did much to promote it, for example in building a public library of books from his church. He was pastor of St. Luke's Lutheran Church until he died in 1898.

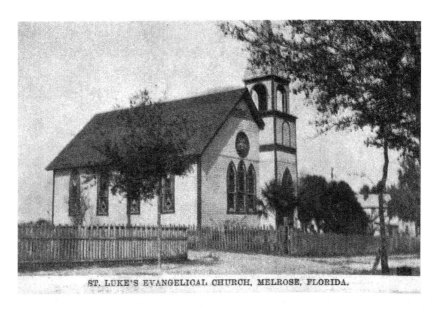

ST. LUKE'S EVANGELICAL CHURCH, MELROSE, FLORIDA.

John McLeod remodeled the church into a private home in the 1920s, and it has remained such.

In the winter of 1895 - 1896, several hard freezes killed off the citrus crops and basically put an end to the tourist business. Many winter residents left and told others in the North about the downturn in the prospects of Melrose. Local house prices fell dramatically and businesses closed. The train service continued for some time, but even they had to stop running when business dried up.

Businesses in Melrose in the 1890s

There were sawmills and even turpentine stills in the area around Melrose, although their exact location has not been determined. Some believe that a turpentine still was on the edge of Santa Fe Lake, but again its location has not been determined. The photo below is apparently of the local Westgaard Sawmill that was owned by the Westgaard Family in Melrose.

The local Westgaard Sawmill

The Westgaard Sawmill around 1890 - Ida Westgaard is in the dog cart. Mrs. P.H. Westgaard and Gertrude Westgaard (a nurse) are sitting on a log. Gertrude Westgaard (Reid) is on a lumber wagon.

Kennie Howard

in her personalized history of Melrose, *Yesterday in Florida*, indicated that her father, **McKendrie Lambdin**, acquired the mill, which was inland some distance from the town, and brought it to Melrose Bay, where **Mr. P.H. Westgaard**, an immigrant from Norway, operated it. Lambdin and his hired workers brought the sawmill from inland by a farmer's wagon over sandy and marshy roads. The sound of the mill's whistle, during the years that it worked, was music to the ears of the local residents because it meant that more and more people were building homes there.

The AA. McRae Store and later the Robinson Store

*Grinding and cooking sugar cane on the Hamlyn property
on Melrose Bay in 1896*

It was **Mr. Westgaard** that **Kennie Howard** in her *Yesterday in Florida* book called "one of the most enthusiastic citizens of the town in the first years of the 1880s." (p. 81)

Another local man, Mr. Judd, built the Trinity Episcopal Church of Melrose on Bellamy between Center Street and Cypress Street. Trinity Episcopal Church was the second church building in Melrose – after the Methodist Church.

When the Episcopal Church building was finished in Melrose around 1896, Reverend Gilmore of Gainesville performed the services, along with his wife, who helped in establishing a ladies' aid society and Sunday school.

59

*Mrs. Lee's millinery shop, seen here perhaps in the 1890s, was
on the first floor of the two-story store building facing
Cypress Street on the northwest corner
of Cypress and Park Streets.*

William Lee, her husband and one of the most important
builders in the early history of the town, built this store building
in the 1880s. The back part of the building was a packing house
where the oranges that Mr. Lee bought were packed and then
shipped north. (See the photo on the bottom of p. 48.) In later
years, Dr. **Paul Lee** had a dental office on the second floor. (For a
photo of the original Lee House, see p. 36.)

*An ad in "Guide
to Melrose, 1894 -
1895" for
Mrs. Lee's shop*

MRS. W. H. LEE,
Choice Millinery and Notions.
Good Line of Trimmed and Untrimmed Hats on Hand.
MELROSE, FLORIDA.

60

Hauling logs to the local sawmill

It took large wheels to haul the heavy logs to the sawmill.

The Vogelbach Pharmacy – Dr. Vogelbach lived on Bellamy Road across from where Blue Water Bay is today. He built his first pharmacy next to his house, but it burned down. Then he built the second one where the Homemakers Club is today. In 1907, Dr. Frank McRae bought it and his daughter, Claudia, operated the business, which was a pharmacy and store. Dr. Frank McRae had his examining room at the back of the building, and the drugstore was at the front. The photo above shows the drugstore, which now houses Historic Melrose, Inc. on the corner of Centre and Park Streets.

The road to Palatka from Melrose was a sandy trail in the 1890s.

The Orr Family

One of the distinguished families that moved to Melrose, at least for the winters in the late 19th century, was the Orr Family. The father, **Nathaniel Orr** (1822-1908), was a well-known engraver of his time. Born in London, Ontario, he learned engraving from **John H. Hall** of Albany, New York, and moved his business to New York City. In 1846, Orr married **Elisabeth Holmes** (1825-1909) of Albany County, New York. She was the author of several books, including *The Belle Heiress* (1849), stories, newspaper and journal articles, and poems. They called their home in Melrose on the bay "Home Acre."

A picture of **Mr. Orr** *fishing from a dock at Home Acre on the Bay*

The Orrs, who had a home in Hohokus, New Jersey, spent many winters in Melrose. They had seven children, but only three, all daughters, survived to adulthood: **Sarah Z. Moore** (b. 1847), **Effie Hamlyn**, and **Alice B. Tredwell** (b. 1860). Effie married an English nobleman, **Walter Hamlyn**, who is the only member of the family buried in Melrose.

Pictured above is the daughter of Sarah Moore: **Elisabeth (Bessie) Holmes Moore** *(1876 – 1959), an American tennis champion who won the singles national championship four times (1896, 1901, 1903, 1905), the women's doubles championship twice (1896, 1903), and the mixed doubles championship twice (1902, 1904).*
She was inducted into the International Tennis Hall of Fame in 1971.

The Literary and Debating Society

In 1890, nine local women organized the Literary and Debating Society in Melrose, first meeting in Rosewood, the home of **Mrs. Elmira Vogelbach**. **Mrs. Eliza King**, a wealthy woman from England who was in the Society, was instrumental in building the clubhouse. She became the first president of the club and donated the land on which the clubhouse was later built. In the early years, the club had many discussions about women's rights. The aim of the Society, as stated in its preamble, was to foster moral, mental, and social culture in its public entertainment and private meetings.

*The above photo shows members of the Melrose
Ladies' Literary and Debating Society around the 1890s.*

The Society members also worked hard to construct a hall where they and other community groups could meet. Under the guidance of **Mr. E.L. Judd**, members planned and built "The Hall."

Finally, in 1893 "The Hall" was completed and handed over to the Society, which held monthly meetings there to discuss current issues and problems. A lending library was opened to the public (more about the library in the "1900" section). Men and women formed a community-wide Improvement Society to beautify the town and improve the sanitary and health conditions.

Among the groups that used the Hall was the Adventist congregation, as well as other community groups that held music recitals, plays, flower shows, receptions for teachers, and suppers. The 1894 – 1895 freeze, the loss of the citrus industry, the decrease in tourism, World War I, and the Great Depression brought many challenges to the Society, but it never disbanded. In 1895 it opened its library to the public. According to **Jessie Meyer**'s *Leading the Way: A Century of Service – The Florida Federation of Women's Clubs, 1895 – 1995*, the clubhouse of the group opened in 1893 and became "the oldest clubhouse in the state that has been in continuous use by a woman's club since it was first opened. (p. 16)

In 1897, the Society joined the Florida Federation of Women Clubs, but withdrew two years later, possibly because the state-wide organization refused to have its annual meeting in Melrose, supposedly because of "travel difficulties." The Society would later rejoin it in 1952.

The original clubhouse

Excursions to Green Cove Springs

The Green Cove Springs and Melrose Railroad (pictured below), not only brought passengers and cargo to Melrose, but also provided an easy means for Melrose residents to spend an enjoyable afternoon enjoying the pleasures of the town north of Melrose on the St. Johns River.

The Green Cove Springs and Melrose Railroad
in the 1890s at Melrose Station

Kennie Howard described in her *Yesterday in Florida* book (p. 151) how many young people made the trip from Melrose to Green Cove Springs for a picnic and a swim in the sulphur waters of the springs there (see a photo of the springs on the next page). The springs brought very hot, sulfur-smelling water out of the earth into a containment area and then into the St. Johns.

So-called "old-timers" in Melrose liked the fact that a train came every day from Green Cove Springs, bringing with it news of others places, as well as visitors. Pictured to the left is an image of Green Cove Springs and its pool.

The engineer, **John Payne**, would often stop the train in the woods on the way back to Melrose to pick up pine knots for train fuel and to allow the passengers a chance to get off the train, stretch their legs, and even pick some wild flowers until the train was ready to finish the trip. It was a very pleasant outing for the Melrosites who made the round-trip.

Postmasters

The Melrose postmasters and their dates in office for the 1890s were **Lucy M. Fox** (July 24, 1889 – May 8, 1893), **Hiram S. Fickle** (May 8, 1893 – May 7, 1895), **Frank Mollas** (May 7, 1895 – June 19, 1897), and **Nathaniel Mullen** (June 19, 1897 – Feb. 27, 1902).

Images of Melrose from the 1890s

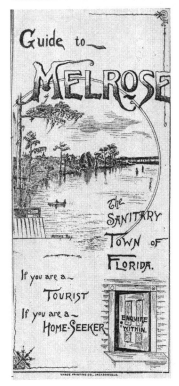

The image to the left shows a bill of lading for shipping out crates of oranges on the Florida Central & Peninsular Railroad Co. in 1891.

The image to the left is of the cover of an 1894 brochure about Melrose, called "The Sanitary Town of Florida." The following pages will show reproductions of pages from that brochure, pages that show a variety of businesses, indicating how well the town was thriving. All that would change dramatically for the worse when the devastating freezes of 1894 – 1895 caused many citrus growers to give up and businesspeople to move elsewhere.

Images of pages from the previously
mentioned brochure about Melrose in 1894

More images from the brochure

And more

Final images from the brochure

Chapter Four: 20th Century

1900s

Officially the town limits were described as "extending one-half of a mile in four directions from the point where the boundaries of Alachua, Clay and Putnam Counties intersect, so as to include an area one mile square." The Clay County line was adjusted several times. For example, the present line was moved one-half mile north of S.R. 26 sometime after 1927.

Melrose was still a small town, as evidenced by the picture here of cows relaxing on Quail Street around 1900, a time of free-ranging animals, unrestricted by fences.

The Melrose Woman's Club, as well as women's clubs throughout Florida, lobbied the Legislature for many years to pass a fence law to get the cows off the public roads of the state. It would not happen until 1948, after **Fuller Warren** was elected Governor of Florida on a promise to convince the Legislature to pass such a law, but wandering cows were still a problem in the 1960s.

The Melrose Inn

The Melrose Inn, seen here perhaps in the early 1900s, was built in 1890 to serve the many expected visitors who would be arriving by boat from the North. It was situated between Park and Pine and Centre Streets.

It later became the Hotel Santa Fe, but then became a military school (Phi Sigma College) when **Mr. George Looney** (pictured to the right), who had moved to the area around 1890, bought it in 1909. It would serve as a military school for two years, until it burned down in 1911.

The pictures below show the military college in Melrose

PHI SIGMA COLLEGE, GEORGE C. LOONEY, PRESIDENT, MELROSE, FLORIDA.

The military cadets of Phi Sigma College in Melrose

Alfred Pearsall Family
—Westfield, NJ
Left to right: J. Herbert, Ruth,
Ralph, Alfred (father), Leigh, &
Grace (wife of Clifford), Clifford

A picture of the Pearsall Family around the 1890s

Leigh Pearsall, who was from Westfield, New Jersey, came to Melrose in 1900 on his honeymoon. His father had been coming to Melrose for about fifteen years in the winter. Leigh started buying property in 1900 in Melrose and continued buying. Pearsall Circle is named after him.

He lived on the lake and owned hundreds of acres on the east side of Santa Fe Lake. He had one daughter, **Edna**. He also had two boats that he called "Dixie" and "The Indian Princess," which is pictured on the next page.

77

"INDIAN PRINCESS," L. M. PEARSALL, OWNER, MELROSE, FLORIDA.

Pearsall's boat, "Indian Princess"

Some of the Pearsall brothers later built homes on the bay. Leigh himself lived in Melrose full time when he retired. At one point he tore his house down, when he retired, and built the house that is still on the property.

In the early 1900s, **Alfred Pearsall**, the father of Leigh, purchased what was called the "Latchstring" property on Melrose Bay. Pearsall was a winter visitor to Melrose during the late 1800s, staying at the Melrose Inn and perhaps at some of the other boarding houses. After buying this house, he and a local carpenter, **Joseph Turnipseed**, made many changes and additions, including the installation of a bay window with two colored-glass windows from his home in the North. The Latchstring is located on Melrose Bay at the end of Latchstring Road.

Alfred Pearsall *(on the left) worked with* **Joseph Turnipseed,**
*a local carpenter (on the right), to expand the Latchstring House
(see below).*

The Latchstring House

The Melrose Inn

In the 1890s - before the fire

In 1911 - during the fire

Pictured above is the Morrison Store, which was built in the 1880s and later bought by **Mr. Coward** *in 1905. It later became the Alex Craig Store at Park and Hampton Streets – where this photo was taken. The building was later torn down.*

The men pictured here in the Morrison Store are (left to right) **Simon Coward, Wilbur Dunbar, Elmer Dunbar**, *and an unidentified man.*

*Two photos
showing when a
carnival came to
town in 1906*

Mr. Whitehead (pictured above near a wagon) was one of the citrus growers who continued growing crops even after the devastating 1894 – 1895 freezes. The photo here shows him in his orange grove – with his home in the back of the photo. He owned about three acres next to **Leigh Pearsall**'s home. The photo shows a wagon full of orange crates, probably on their way to the local dock, where the product would be sent by boat to Waldo.

A local Woodmen of the World Dinner in Melrose

The Woodmen of the World was an organization founded in 1890 in Nebraska that operated a privately held insurance company for its members. The picture below shows local women acting as waitresses at a turtle soup dinner for members of the Woodmen of the World.

The waitresses at the "Turtle Supper" at the Town Hall in 1908:
Left to right: 1st step: **Sadie Mullin** *(or* **Mullen***),*
Flora Morris, Claudia McRae*;*
2nd step: **Eva Priest, Kate Mizell***;*
3rd step: **Cara Lyons, Nettie Huffman,**
May Barnett*,* **Laurie Stokes***;*
Top: **Stella Coward, Emma Baldwin**

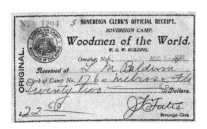

The 1907 membership card
of Melrosian resident
L.M. Baldwin

Incorporation

The town of Melrose was incorporated from January 21, 1902 until c. 1914, at which point – for reasons that are not clear – officials unincorporated the town. The first officials were as follows: mayor: Dr. **Frank McRae**; councilmen: **L.M. Baldwin, J.A. Board, W.H. Lee, A.A. McRae**, and **Wm. Vogelbach**; town clerk: **H. Jackson**; town marshal: **Simon Coward**.

For the next twelve years the following men served as councilmen, as well: **L.M. Baldwin, O.C. Husband, Simon Coward, A.W. Craig, Fred Ford, John Hilton, C.P. Huffman, V.L. Mack, A.G. McGregor, Charles Nobles, N.E. Priest** (who was the clerk for many years), **Hans Von Noszky** (who was mayor for many years), and **W. Yearwood**.

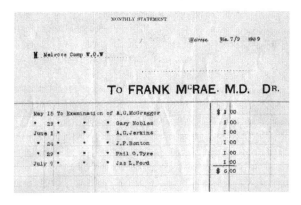

A monthly statement from Dr. **Frank McRae** *in 1909*

Post Office

The second post office in Melrose, was in Husband's general store on Bellamy Road.

Postmasters

The Melrose postmasters and their dates in office for the 1900s were **Nathaniel Mullen** (June 19, 1897 – Feb. 27, 1902), **Margaret E. Mullen** (Feb. 27, 1902 – July 30, 1907), **Sadie L. Mullen** (July 30, 1907 – July 14, 1909), and **Orville C. Husband** (July 14, 1909 – Jan. 31, 1931).

Schools in Melrose

According to the Clay County Archives, which gave us permission to reproduce the photo here of the Melrose Academy and the one on the next page, a school was begun in 1878 in an old gin house with principal Prof. **C.C. Hill** of Louisville, Kentucky. Two years later, **W.N. Sheats**, the County Superintendent of Alachua County, held a meeting of concerned citizens to discuss the issue of constructing a new school building.

The following men were appointed to investigate the matter: **H. Alderman, J.M. Barnett, Alex. Goodson, Mr. Hawkins, Frank McRae, John McRae, "Wash" McRae, John Wolf,** and Dr. **H.A. Vogelbach**. Mr. and Mrs. **Joseph Lynn** donated six acres of land in Melrose and workers put up the building in 1882.

The Melrose Academy

The building, valued at $3,000, had six rooms and a large hall with a stage, music rooms, and recitation rooms. It was in the Clay County section of Melrose, but today may be in the Putnam County section. The Masonic fraternity laid the cornerstone. Over one hundred of its graduates became teachers in Florida public schools, and it had the distinction of having only one of its students fail in a teachers' examination. The principals were professors **C.V. Waugh**, **G.C. Looney**, and **G. M. Lynch**.

The school pictured below was labeled Melrose Negro School No. 4. The image also comes from the Clay County Archives.

Melrose Negro School No. 4

The Clay County line was adjusted several times. The present line was moved a half mile north of S.R. 26 sometime after 1927.

People of Melrose

Leigh Pearsall's *home in the early 1900s –*
he and his family would play an important role in the early
development of Melrose, for example in advertising the town
in publications in the North. Also see p. 109 for a photo of the palm
nursery Mr. Pearsall planted on Seminole Ridge Road.

A scene of
people at
the Melrose Inn

Martha MacDonald, *an ex-slave who worked for*
Leigh Pearsall, *at her cabin near the Punch Bowl Lake*
in Melrose. The Devil's Punch Bowl was so called
because it looked like a punch bowl
and because a young girl drowned there.

Kennie Howard in her *Yesterday in Florida* book (p. 61) wrote that a number of African-American families lived in the area, for example families with the names **Brown, Homes, Kirkland, Lewis, Pelham, Pilcher**, and **Tutson**, They were good workers that could be relied on. A number of the African Americans, who had been slaves before the Civil War, took their masters' names when the war freed the slaves.

One of the hard jobs that **McKendrie "Mac" Lambdin** hired African Americans for was to transport a sawmill from back in the woods in sections to the foot of Trout Street, and there it remained for several years and became very useful to those building homes in the new community.

*A photo of the seventh birthday party on October 9, 1903,
for Melrose resident **Neva Husband** (front row, fifth from the left).
The last two girls in the first row on the far right are the **Lee sisters**.*

**Neva
Husband**
*and her
father,
postmaster*
**Orville
Husband**,
around 1903

The Melrose Public Library

History of the Melrose Public Library and Melrose Library Association

As discussed in this book's chapter dealing with the 1890s, the Literary and Debating Society opened a lending library to the public.

Also the Reverend **A.H. Waters**, the local Lutheran minister, had his own lending library in town.

The *History of the Melrose Public Library and Melrose Library Association* detailed the long history of the institution and how important it has been to the community.

Then in 1900, the Reverend **George Gilmore** of Trinity Episcopal Church contacted the Society for the Propagation of Christian Knowledge, a group in England, which sent two cases of books to Melrose. Reverend Gilmore stored the books at the church since the town did not have a library building yet.

Others in the community donated more books, which the church lent out to people there. **Emma Brinson**, the daughter of Trinity's senior warden, did much to encourage the community to support the library. (More about the library in the "1930" section.)

Local Inventor

In 1907, **Dewitt Miller** of Melrose invented and secured a patent for a bricklayer's mitt (see picture to the left). The mitt protected the ends of the fingers of bricklayers and those who handled bricks and similar objects that "have a tendency to quickly wear off the skin of the ends of the fingers and in this way make them sore." The mitts protected the ends of the fingers while at the same time keeping the hand open for work.

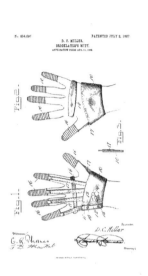

Dewitt Miller also patented what was called a "Railway joint chair" in 1909, referring to a method of railway rail joints. It is also called a "fishplate" and refers to the metal bar that is joined to the ends of two rails to fasten them together. Above is a picture of a modern fishplate.

Melrose Jail

Pictured above is a building that was used as the Melrose jail, but no longer exists. It was southwest of the Methodist Church and was used in the early 1900s, when the town was incorporated for a short time.

The story goes that out-of-towners would come to town on Saturday, get drunk, and get into fights, at which point a local official would throw them into the jail. On Monday morning, a deputy sheriff would come to town and take them to court in Gainesville. The jail lasted only a few years. (See p. 97 for a typical list of cases on the court docket.)

1910s

Harry Jackson was a Melrose resident who did much for the town, including the sale of caskets, which he stored in the second floor of the Baldwin Store. He built a small train that could take tourists from Melrose to Orange Heights around 1915.

HARRY JACKSON,
CARRIAGE AND WAGON BUILDER
AND UNDERTAKER,
MELROSE, - - - - - - FLORIDA.

An ad for **Harry Jackson** *in the local newspaper*

The **Greenberry Jackson** *House, built in 1877, had additions done to it in 1890, 1980, and 1990. His son,* **Harry Jackson**, *married* **Ruth Goodson** *and they had two children:* **Harry** *and* **Harriett**. *Three generations of the Jacksons have continued to live in the house.*

Harry Jackson*'s car could carry five trunks for visitors.*

The picture above shows the Harry Jackson train that went to Orange Heights. The railroad was on South Street two blocks south of S.R. 26 (Bellamy Road).

95

A picture of the time that **Harry Jackson**'s
home-made train jumped the tracks near Orange Heights.

The names of some of the people around the train off the tracks: left of train: **Alfred Pearsall** (white pants). Right of train: **Harry Jackson**. Jackson was a real "jack-of-all-trades. He operated a power company, a water company, a freight boat, a garage, a blacksmith shop, an ice house, and a place that embalmed the dead and sold caskets. He also built carriages and wagons and taxied salesmen around town.

Board of Trade of Melrose

The Board of Trade of Melrose was organized in March, 1911 with the following officers: **E.J. Whitehead**, president; **Frank McRae**, vice-president; **A.A. McRae**, secretary; and **H. Von Noszky**, treasurer.

The Lambdins around 1910

Left to right:
McKendrie, Charles Weber, *and* **Ella**
2nd row: **Bertha Weber** *and* **Kennie Lambdin Howard**

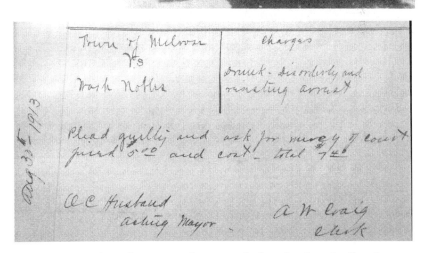

A typical list of cases on the town docket that local officials dealt with is from 1913.

The local post office and general store

Orville Husband *(postmaster from 1909 to 1931) and his wife,* **Sara (Renshaw) Husband**, *ran a post office and general store (seen above) on S.R. 26 (Bellamy Road) in Melrose.*

Mr. & Mrs. **Orville Husband** *in their store/post office*

An outing on the lake

The people in the above photograph have been identified as follows: on the bow: **Edna Pearsall Cooper***; on the roof, l to r:* **Bill Hutchings** *and* **Walter Hamlyn***; on the dock left to right:* **Hans von Nostzky (?)**, **Mrs. Hans von Nostzky**, **Mrs. E.J. Whitehead**, **Mrs. Hutchings**, **Mrs. Walter (Effie) Hamlyn**, **Mrs. Alice Treadwell**, **Mrs. Harriet Pearsall**, **Mrs. Leigh Pearsall***, and* **Mr. E.J. Whitehead**

The boat in the photograph was one of several that Mr. **Leigh Pearsall** owned, one of which was the "Indian Princess." This particular photograph was probably taken on Little Santa Fe Lake.

Another photo of Mr. **Orville Husband** *in his store/post office*

The Town Square in 1910 at Bellamy and Hampton

*Two boys (***Robert** *and* **Morgan Pearsall***) at Davis
Railroad Depot on South Street in 1913*

*The memorial in Heritage Park that honors local residents
who served in World War I (1914 – 1918) - see Appendix
at the back of the book for a list of those veterans and see the
next page for a picture of the draft card of a local man.*

*The draft card
for Alex Nobles
of Melrose*

*(Below:) The Baldwin
Store in 1916*

*The list on the upper left-hand side of the store's stationery indicates
what lines the store could handle: dry goods, notions, shoes, clothing,
hats, staple groceries, drugs, glassware, hardware, stoves, trunks and
bags, furniture, matting and rugs, paints, oils, etc. The Baldwin Store
sold caskets on the second floor.*

Two local men killed as police detectives in Jacksonville

Napoleon B. Hagan, *who was born February 14, 1871 in Melrose and married* **Mattie Lee Phillips** *in 1899, moved his family to Jacksonville, Florida, in 1911 and joined the Jacksonville Police Department. He was fatally shot by a burglar on September 15, 1913 and died eight days later. His name is inscribed on the National Law Enforcement Memorial in Washington, DC (East Wall, Panel 53, Line 7).*

Benjamin Franklin Hagan, *who was born on January 10, 1873 near Melrose and who married* **Mary Ann Crosby** *on April 1, 1894, joined the Jacksonville Police Department around 1908. Nine years later, on August 6, 1917, he was fatally shot while attempting to arrest an armed robber and died four days later. His name is inscribed on the National Law Enforcement Memorial in Washington, DC. (East Wall, Panel 58, Line 13).*

An Eliam Baptist Church baptism
on Quail Street on the Bay in 1918

Postmaster
The Melrose postmaster and his dates in office for the 1910s were **Orville C. Husband** (July 14, 1909 – Jan. 31, 1931).

Kennie Howard's Yesterday in Florida *book tells us much about the history of Melrose up to 1946.*

1920s

In 1922, **Mrs. Virginia Aycock** sold Bayview to **Mrs. Zella A. King** and her husband, **W.W. King**, a retired turpentine operator from Marion County, Florida. The King Family lived in Bayview until 1929.

In 1929, **Mr. and Mrs. Windsor H. Wyman** from Plymouth County, Massachusetts, bought Bayview and improved it. Mrs. Wyman was president of the Melrose Woman's Club and increased its membership and encouraged the club in many community projects.

The "City of Melrose" at the Waldo dock

El Robinson owned the "City of Melrose" and used it to transport freight to the railroad in Waldo up until the 1920s, when roads made transportation much easier in Florida.

Businesses in Melrose

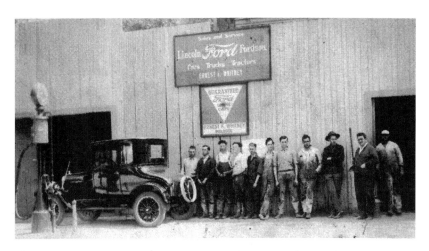

The Lincoln Ford Car Dealer in Melrose was located on Bellamy Road and Cypress Street where Heritage Park is today. **Ernest Whitney**, *the owner of the business, is the fifth from the right in the above photo. The staff sold cars and also repaired them there.*

Pastor John Minder of Melrose

A pastor in Melrose, Rev. **John Minder**, was serving there in 1922 when he secured property east of the town on nearby Lake Swan in Putnam County. According to an article by **Lois Ferm** in the *Florida Historical Quarterly*, Rev. Minder acquired the property at Lake Swan for his Bible conference activities and held the first conference there in 1927 and continued to expand its activities from then on. Besides his work in Melrose, he served as the special adviser and counselor to Rev. **Billy Graham** at the beginning of the latter's career. (For more about this see the mini-chapter on the 1930s.)

Buildings from the 1920s

In the 1920s, Miss **Annie Harper**, a religious leader from New Jersey, built the non-denominational church on Grove Street between Bellamy Ave. and Pearl Street. The large frame church with stucco exterior had stained-glass windows, which were originally in the Melrose Lutheran Church. The church was later sold and became Anne Lowry Antiques and later Mossman Hall.

Annie Harper and **Mary Mossman**, who lived in the adjacent house, in the 1920s had the church built, where they held nonsectarian services.

The non-denominational church

The Lee House

William Lee, a builder who built many of the early homes in Melrose, built and lived in what may be the third-oldest house in the town, dating to 1879 (see p. 36 for a photo of that house). He

and his family lived in the house, pictured above, while it was being built between Park and Cypress. His wife, **Alice**, the former **Sarah Alice Alderman**, and their month-old baby, **Paul**, were living in the town when the Clay County Census was taken in 1880. (Pictured to the right are Mr. and Mrs. Lee.)

William kept enlarging his house as his family grew. His wife operated the structure as a boarding house in the 1890s, and members of the Lee Family lived in the house for over one hundred years.

108

Postmaster

The Melrose postmaster and his dates in office for the 1920s were **Orville C. Husband** (July 14, 1909 – Jan. 31, 1931).

People of Melrose

H. Walter Hamlyn
and **Edna Hamlyn**

According to **Kennie Howard** *in her* Yesterday in Florida *book, Walter chose the name Devonia Street, on which* **Walter** *and* **Effie Orr** *(his first wife) lived, after his home in England.* **H. Walter Hamlyn** *is the only one of the* **Orr Family** *who is buried in the Melrose Cemetery. The rest are buried in the Orr Family plot in New Jersey.*

Leigh Pearsall'*s palm nursery on Seminole Ridge Road about 1920*

109

*Melrose in the first part of the twentieth century
had dirt roads and a simple welcome sign.*

Melrose School, part two

In 1927, Melrose High School moved to its present location when Putnam County built a new wooden building with a
stucco exterior-finish for grades one through twelve. Workers used
wood from the 1882 school building for construction of the new
gymnasium.

The Melrose School gymnasium as pictured in 1934

110

1930s

Melrose Public Library

As discussed in the parts dealing with the 1890s and 1900s, a number of Melrosians felt that a public library would be an important addition to the town. As described in the "History of the Melrose Public Library and Melrose Library Association," the Reverend **Fred Yerkes** (pictured to the left) of Trinity Episcopal Church in 1939 encouraged the local Boy Scouts to build a small hut on the church grounds for meetings. That hut became the repository for the books of the lending library. But when local officials applied for federal library assistance from the Works Progress Administration (WPA), they moved the books from the Boy Scout hut to what is now the Melrose Homemakers Club for about five years.

The Homemakers Club

Chiappini's Gas Station

In 1935, "**Papa Joe**" **Chiappini** built Chiappini's Gas Station, which his descendants run today. After immigrating from Italy to the United States in the early 1900s to work in the New York City area, Papa Joe met **Leigh Pearsall**, who lived in Melrose in the winter. After a stint in the U.S. Army in World War I, Joe moved to Melrose to become the caretaker of the Pearsall properties. He later acquired land from Pearsall and built his store on the corner of S.R. 26 and S.R. 21.

Postmasters

The Melrose postmasters and their dates in office for the 1930s were **Orville C. Husband** (July 14, 1909 – Jan. 31, 1931), **Olive B. Lunsden** (Jan. 31 – 1931 – April 6, 1931), and **Frank B. Stewart** (April 6, 1931 – May 15, 1956).

The so-called "Melrose Bowlers" bowled on the green at Hamlyn's. Pictured here in 1935 they are left to right: **Edwards, Harned, Love, Hamlyn, Brown, Forster, Dunbar, Potter**. *They also played golf (three holes) on the street near Hamlyn's home.*

The Melrose School and Gymnasium

Melrose School, pictured in 1934: an elementary school was built on this site around 1927. The Mediterranean-revival style of the 1920s building was reproduced after it burned in 1945.

Third Baptist Church in 1926

Lee Brothers Found Dead in Their Home

A double tragedy occurred to the Lee Brothers in 1936. One brother, Dr. **Paul H. Lee**, age 55, had a heart attack in January and died. His brother, **Robert Ernest Lee**, age 54, found the body of his brother and then killed himself with a pistol, falling over the body of his dead brother.

Authorities in Palatka were notified by phone, and Sheriff **Hancock** and Judge **C.S. Green** were called to the scene to investigate, but found that no inquest was necessary. A newspaper article about the deaths noted about the suicide of Robert: "Apparently through grief over finding his brother cold in death, the younger had taken his own life." Double funeral services for the two brothers were held in January, 1936, in Melrose.

At the time, three brothers (Dr. **Paul H.**, **Robert Ernest**, and **Homer**) and two sisters (**Addie** and **Anna**) all lived in the house. Two other siblings were **Mrs. O.R. Ingram** of Boston, Georgia and Captain **John Lee** of Mobile, Alabama.

The Lee House in Melrose in 2016

Melrose and Rev. Billy Graham

An unusual connection between Melrose and the great preacher, **Billy Graham**, occurred in 1938. At that time, Reverend **John Minder**, who had served a church in Melrose in 1922 and who acquired land at Lake Swan (see 1920s mini-chapter), drove with Rev. Graham to a conference in Palatka. According to an article by **Lois Ferm** in the *Florida Historical Quarterly*, Rev. Minder and Billy Graham visited there a part-time Baptist minister, **Cecil Underwood**, who was scheduled to preach that day in the small town of Bostwick north of Palatka.

Rev. **Billy Graham**
later in his career

At the last minute, Rev. Underwood declined to give the sermon and insisted that Rev. Minder take his place, but the latter asked Billy Graham to take his place even though Rev. Graham had very little experience preaching up to that point, having spoken mostly on street corners in Tampa. Billy Graham agreed to preach in Bostwick, but spoke so quickly that he finished four small sermons in a relatively short time. However, he did so well that it was the beginning of a long, very distinguished career of preaching in churches.

Golf in Melrose

Thanks to communication from **Hugh A. Barnett, Jr.**, we know about golf in Melrose in the 1920s and 1930s. The "golf course" was basically a relatively small one laid out in the dirt roadways and so-called "sidewalk" areas, mostly along Pine Street.

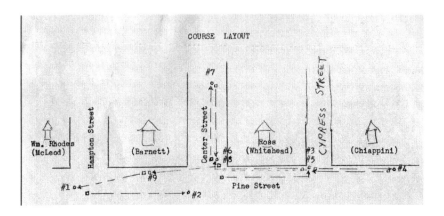

A rough sketch showing the lay-out of the golf course in the 1930s

Play began around 1928 and continued for about ten years. The holes were embedded tin cans. The shortest hole (#1) was but 135 feet, and the longest (#2) was about 180 feet. See the sketch above, although it is not drawn to scale. The indicated par (three par 4s and six par 3s) may sound rather high for such short holes.

On the sketch above the first "tee" and the ninth hole were near the side of the Barnett House. Play angled west and a bit south to a tin can embedded in the middle of the road area that ran past the McLeod Home.

116

Initial efforts to make golf clubs of suitably shaped tree limbs soon gave way to the use of small blocks of wood drilled to accept broom-handle shafts. The clubs were upgraded when the father of **Hugh Barnett, Jr.**, while at his former home in Miami, bought four brassies (#2 woods) on sale in a hardware store for a dollar each. He offered three dollars for all four, an offer that the store keeper accepted. From then on, the Melrose golfers chipped and putted with real golf clubs.

Scores were usually in the 26 – 32 range, with the record possibly 22 or 23. When an occasional hole-in-one was made, **Mr. McLeod** would yells "HOLE!" loud enough to be heard two blocks away. Later, when Mr. McLeod's eyesight had begun to fade, after a close shot he would ask: "Shall I holler? Shall I holler?"

In the mid-1930s Melrose had at least one regular course golfer: **Mr. Yates**, a retired administrator living at the Santa Fe Inn and a member of the Keystone Heights Club's nine-hole, sand-green course.

1940s

Kennie Howard in her *Yesterday in Florida* book (p. 69) wrote that a **Mrs. Wyman** and another lady found out in 1946 that Front Street was originally Trout Street, named after **Robert "Bob" Trout**, a local businessman who operated a livery stable on his namesake street.

For some reason, "Trout" was changed to "Front," but the two enterprising women drove to the courthouse, probably in Gainesville, and officially had the name changed back to "Trout."

Bob Trout had gone to a town in South Florida that became Miami after the 1894 – 1895 freezes did much damage to the fields around Melrose, but he is still honored with a local street name.

Another street misspelling, according to **Kennie Howard** in her *Yesterday in Florida* book, concerned modern-day Grove  Street, which used to be Green Street. For some reason, "Green" became "Grove," which it is today.

Melrose Fire Department

Fire-fighting has been a long-time concern of the residents of Melrose, especially because the fire-fighting equipment of Gainesville and other towns was quite distant in terms of time to reach the scene of a fire in Melrose.

In 1948, the Melrose Fire Department bought for $600 a 1942 Ford truck with a 600-gallon tank and a pump capable of delivering eight hundred pounds of pressure. The truck had formerly been used for spraying fruit trees. Fire chief **Ralph Matthews** of the Fire Department arranged for the public to view the fire-fighting capability of the truck at Whitney's Garage. Officials estimated that it would cost $1,500 for the truck and other fire-fighting equipment: chemical equipment, hose, nozzles, etc.

A picture of Melrose's first fire truck - in 1948

Officials were going to canvass Melrose and surrounding areas to a distance of three miles for contributions to buy the truck and its equipment. **Harry Huffman** was elected treasurer of the Fire Department to handle the money donations.

The picture above shows the fire truck and a volunteer fireman standing in front of the large iron ring that someone would ring at the first sign of fire in the town. Volunteer firemen would rush to the fire house and go off to fight the fire.

Because Melrose is in four counties, officials in those counties have been reluctant to spend a lot of money on fire-fighting equipment for a fire that was not in their own county. For example, in 2016, Alachua County officials, arguing that only forty percent of the town's fires were actually in Alachua County, cut its funding to the Melrose Fire Department to reflect the county's share of service calls. At that time (2016), the fire department had two employed firefighters and ten volunteers.

A picture of **Frank Stewart,**
postmaster of Melrose from 1931 to 1956;

Postmaster

The Melrose postmaster and his dates in office for the 1940s were **Frank B. Stewart** (April 6, 1931 – May 15, 1956).

Military Families

When wives of the soldiers at Camp Blanding came to visit them, they would stay in Melrose, for example at the Lee House. There was no movie hall or dance hall in Melrose in the 1940s, but the town was relatively close to the military base.

Some of the military at Camp Blanding, especially the officers, including the commander of the base, bought houses around Melrose Bay, and some of those military families retired here. The town started to grow after World War II.

Melrose School, part three

In 1945, after fire damaged the Melrose School, the Board of Public Instruction made plans to keep students from missing school days: classes for the first and second graders were held in Melrose Methodist Church, third and fourth in the Episcopal Boy Scout House, and fifth and sixth grades in the Woman's Club-house. Classes for seventh through twelfth were held in the Eliam Baptist Church basement. It took a year-and-a-half to rebuild the school using the original 1927 building plans.

Melrose School as seen in 2016

Near the school is one of four state historic markers in Melrose.

Melrose Public Library, continued

The books that would become part of the town's public library were moved from their temporary housing in the Boy Scout hut around 1939 to what had been McRae's Drugstore. The books remained there for about five years.

When the federal money ran out, officials moved the books back to Trinity Episcopal Church, which by that time had a parish house.

History of the Melrose Public Library and Melrose Library Association

Volunteers moved the books to the loft of that parish house. However, when the stairs became a problem for some of the library patrons, volunteers moved the books back to the Boy Scout hut.

The Scouts agreed to hold their meetings, not in the hut, but in the church parish house. (More about the public library in the "1950s" section.)

The building that housed the books for about five years had been McRae's Drugstore from around 1909 until the owner died around the 1940s. In 1952, it became the Homemakers Club. Historic Melrose, Inc., was deeded the building in 2002.

The memorial in Heritage Park that honors
the local residents who fought in World War II (1939 to 1945).
For the list of veterans from the Melrose area who served
in World War II, see the appendix at the back of this book.

1950s

Melrose Woman's Club

In 1952, the local Melrose branch of the Literary and Debating Society joined the Florida Federation of Women's Clubs, from which it had withdrawn fifty years before. The local group changed their name to the Melrose Woman's Club. The club has continued to be a strong presence in the community, sponsoring groups of Boy Scouts and Brownie troops, awarding scholarships

to high school graduates, offering sickroom supplies to residents and those in outlying communities, offering a health and dental-care program for needy school children, and financing in 1968 a pilot breakfast program at the school.

Bellamy Road (S.R. 26) and Grove Street in Melrose in the 1950s was still relatively free of businesses.

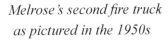

Melrose's second fire truck as pictured in the 1950s

125

The Melrose Post Office in 1953 was on the southeast corner of Bella-my Road and Hampton Street. **Mr. Whitney**, *who owned the building, also had a pecan business. The Melrose Post office had many directors over the years - it seemed to be a training office for such directors.*

Melrose Public Library, continued

The successor to the Literary and Debating Society, which was formed in the 1890s, was the Melrose Woman's Club. That club in 1956 persuaded Putnam County officials to pay for a local librarian in Melrose. The first librarian was **Mildred Spires**, who belonged to Trinity Episcopal Church. Other librarians, who worked in the Boy Scout hut, were **Jean Allen** and **Olive Hulett**, also members of Trinity. (More about the public library in the "1970s" section.)

In 1957, **Russell Keener**, son of Mrs. **Kennie L. Howard**, bought Bayview for his mother. Bayview remained in the Keener Family until Mrs. Howard died in 1975 at the age of 94.

In the 1950s, the Melrose Junior Woman's Club bought land on the bay to operate Melrose Beach as a swimming area.

Melrose Beach on Melrose Bay

Postmaster

The Melrose postmasters and their dates in office for the 1950s were **Frank B. Stewart** (April 6, 1931 – May 15, 1956) and **Mary F. McGee** (May 15, 1956 - May 7, 1973).

1960s

Hawthorne Reporter - April, 1969

Melrose Pioneer Likes The Quiet Country Life

By LYLE G. VAN BUSSUM
Tampa Tribune Staff Writer

(Reprint from Tampa Tribune)

— Trade secrets are among the least important things in the life of Walter Hamlyn Mann, who has spent more than three decades doing electrical and plumbing work hereabouts.

"One of my small pleasures is showing people how to make their own repairs, so they can fend for themselves when I pass on," said the 73-year-old native.

Like others his age, Mann wants to retire to his garden, citrus and fish more frequently in Santa Fe Lake.

Last year he tried to hang up his tools of trade and erected a sign (since blown down) advertising his franchised dealerships and business for sale.

"My customers won't let me and don't want me to quit," he said, blue eyes twinkling and face wrinkling in a proud smile.

A seven-day work week is nothing unusual and since he's still in good physical condition, Mann doesn't mind too much answering "not unusual" middle-of-the-night calls for help.

He admits his joints have gotten "a little creaky" in his elder years "and I've given up crawling under low-floored houses" to make repairs.

Photo by Lyle Van Bussum

Mann of Melrose
. . . civilization crowds in on Walter H. Mann

Occasional newspaper articles about Melrose and/or some of its residents, like the 1969 article in the Hawthorne Reporter about 73-year-old **Walter Hamlyn Mann** *shown here, made outsiders know more about the town. Many readers would visit the town to see its attributes for themselves*

In the 1960s, the main road in town was widened and paved, and sidewalks were added.

In 1963, Miss **Marguerita Float** of Melrose High School won first place at the annual meeting of the Florida Historical Society for a paper entitled "The History of Melrose."

Postmasters
The Melrose postmasters and their dates in office for the 1960s were **Mary F. McGee** (May 15, 1956 - May 7, 1973).

1970s

Melrose Arts & Crafts Festival

In 1972, a small group called the Melrose Action Committee began organizing an arts and crafts festival to display the many talents of local artists and craftsmen. The Melrose Community School offered its gymnasium and grounds as a venue for the festival, which took place on the first Saturday of October, 1972. The festival, which did not charge a fee for those exhibiting their art, was meant to benefit the artists, but they also donated money for good causes, for example a school in South Florida that had been damaged in a hurricane in 1992.

A t-shirt for the arts and crafts festival

The committee raised money for expenses by having bake sales, rummage sales, t-shirt sales, and festival cookbook sales. The festival increased in size from having twenty-five participants in its first year to 150 in later years. When the Melrose Action Committee decided to disband and stop sponsoring the festival after doing so for twenty years, the Melrose Business Association, Inc., began conducting the festival and also charging a fee to participate, but the new festival lasted only two years.

The Melrose Centennial Celebration

The Melrose Centennial Celebration took place in May, 1976. To celebrate the nation's 200th anniversary, the residents of Melrose had many activities which attracted hundreds of visitors. The activities included historical tours, arts and crafts displays, horse races like the original Shakerag races (see p. 34), and a colorful parade with floats, bands, decorated cars, as well as barbecue dinners, games, and movies. The Melrose Fire Department was kept busy from 5 p.m. to 7 p.m. as its volunteers served hamburgers and drinks as part of the celebration. `

*The Melrose Fire Station, built in 1974, was busy
in the evening of the celebration.*

Scenes from the 1976 Bicentennial Celebration

Competitors in the "Best Beard Contest"

Members of the Melrose Judo Club in the parade

Scenes from the 1976 Bicentennial Celebration parade

The Melrose Fire Department float

The Betsy Ross float

Girl Scout Troop 418

Parade Marshals Ruth & General Bob Hollis

More Scenes from the 1976 Bicentennial Celebration

Another truck-float

Jerry Bolden

Martha and Lynn TenEyk

Representatives of the Melrose Woman's Club

English Madrigal Dinners in Melrose

Beginning in 1974, several groups in Melrose, including Faith Presbyterian Church, Trinity Episcopal Church, the Melrose Woman's Club, and the American Association of Retired Persons, joined together to put on English madrigal dinners, transporting the attendees several centuries back in time.

The performers staged the dinners to an audience of over one hundred guests on each of three nights. The dinners were held at the "Great Hall" of the Trinity Episcopal Parish House. Court herald **Murray Sipprell** announced the guests as they entered the hall, which was festooned with candelabra, portraits of members of the queen's court, and banners that had the royal coat of arms.

A scene from Melrose's English Madrigal Dinners

English Madrigal Dinners, cont.

Trumpets announced the entrance of the Madrigal singers, who entertained the guests. Music was performed by troubadours **David Benson** and **Bobby Neale**. Post-dinner Madrigal songs were rendered by **Grace Barbot**, **Jack Janes**, **Oonagh Kater**, and **Ray Rood**, while **David Benson**, **Elisa Neale**, and **Lynn TenEyck** played musical selections. Other participants were **Jo Benson**, **Elizabeth Neale**, and **Jimmy Neale**. Merlin the Magician, played by **Joe Daurer**, entertained the audience. The entertainers and members of the court were resplendent in period costumes. The director of the whole evening was **David Benson**, and the producers were **Martha TenEyck** and **Pamela Whiting**.

Photos from the Gilbert and Sullivan operettas performed in Melrose in 1978. Local performers also put on Broadway reviews in 1979. The Melrose Music Theater had productions from 1974 until about 2006.

The 1977 Melrose Centennial Celebration

The 1976 bicentennial celebration was a prelude to the 1977 celebration in Melrose of the founding of the town one hundred years before: in May, 1877. The festivities included a slide show of old and present Melrose, country music bands, and a pageant of early Melrose written by local author **Zonira "Zee" Tolles**, who published her *Shadows on the Sand: A history of the land and the people in the vicinity of Melrose, Florida*, in 1976.

MELROSE CENTENNIAL

1877   Melrose, Florida   **1977**

May 14, 1977

Parade - GRAND OPENING

Food - FRIED CHICKEN DINNER-HAMBURGERS-HOT DOGS-PIES-CAKES-CANDY-DRINKS

Games - FOR ADULTS & CHILDREN

Entertainment - ALL DAY LONG

Pageant - STORY OF OLD MELROSE

Horse Racing - ADULTS & YOUTH

Arts and Crafts - WIDE VARIETY

Antique Show - MELROSE ANTIQUES

Tour of Homes SIX EARLY MELROSE HOMES OPEN

The schedule of events for the Melrose Centennial

Rosemary *and* **Joe Daurer** *in front of a sign for their "Old-time Melrose" slide show at the fire station*

Melrose Centennial Celebration Parade

A group of old cars honoring the first settlers

Some participants rode horses in the parade and participated in the the Shakerag races.

139

Onlookers along the parade route

*Some reenacted the Shakerag horse races
from the early days of Banana.*

One of the participants in the celebration was local resident Zonira Hunter Tolles, *author of two books about the history of Melrose:* Shadows on the Sand: A History of the Land and the People in the Vicinity of Melrose, Florida *(1976) and* Bonnie Melrose: The Early History of Melrose, Florida *(1982).*

One of the houses that visitors could tour as part of the celebration was Bayview, one of the earliest houses built in Melrose.

Three local men in the library (Boy Scout Hut) were part of the 1977
Melrose Centennial Celebration:
Ernest Whitney *(on the left, former owner*
of the Ford dealership in town in the 1920s),
Charlie Huffman *(son of the man who owned*
the Melrose Inn before it became a military academy),
and **Walter Mann** *(on the right,*
a local businessman).

Rudolph Dampier *was the long-time fire*
chief of the Melrose Fire Department
from 1969 to 1991. Rudolph's wife, **Thelma**,
a certified EMT, handled the rescue unit.
The Dampiers conducted both
firefighting and EMT courses.

Historical Marker Dedication

State Representative **Sid Martin** of Hawthorne
with Woman's Club President **Mabel Faikel**

In April, 1977, officials dedicated a state historic marker at the Melrose Woman's Club. Club member **Gwen Bachman**, in giving a history of the Melrose Woman's Club and the efforts to procure the state marker, paid special recognition to the hard work that **Maud Watkins** had done. Ms. Bachman noted that the original hall could be rented out in the 1890s for between twenty-five cents and one dollar in order to raise money for the organization.

Workers finished the interior of the building and added heat after the severe freeze of 1894. Four years later an annex was finished that housed the kitchen and back area of the building. In 1977, the original kerosene lamps were still on the walls, helping to retain a tie to the beginning of the club. In 1990, they celebrated their 100th anniversary. (See page 145 for more information about the building.)

Protecting Area Lakes

Here Today, Here Tomorrow

The Lake Lover's
Guide to
the Santa Fe Lakes

Beginning in the late 1970s, area residents became increasingly concerned about the threats to Melrose Bay, Santa Fe Lake, and Little Santa Fe Lake.

As outlined in the brochure pictured here, "Here Today, Here Tomorrow: The Lake Lover's Guide to the Santa Fe Lakes," enough residents were encouraged to form and join two strong advocacy groups, as outlined in the following pages: Santa Fe Lake Dwellers Association, Inc. and LAKEWATCH.

Residents were determined to learn as much as possible about such problems as the fluctuation of water levels in the lakes, threats to shoreline vegetation, and the best means to provide habitat and food for wildlife and fish, as well as prevent bank erosion along the edges of the lakes.

Many were determined to maintain natural vegetation in order to protect the many species of birds, both permanent and migratory, and to protect the many mammals (bats, beavers, deer, opossums, rabbits, skunks, and squirrels), reptiles, and amphibians that live in or near the lakes.

The building of the Melrose Woman's Club was added to the U.S. National Register of Historic Places in 1978. Founded in 1890 as the Literary and Debating Society, the organization built what came to be known as "The Hall." The building is well-preserved and continues to serve the community with timely programs. (See p. 65 for more about the original Society.) Today the building is the oldest Woman's Club building in Florida.

Melrose Public Library, continued

As interest in a local public library grew in the town **Maud Watkins**, a former principal of Melrose Elementary School, in 1979 went to the State Legislature and – with the help of the local delegation to the Legislature – obtained a state grant that would match funds raised locally. The resulting library was the first full-service branch library in Putnam County. (More about the public library in the "1980s" section.)

Postmasters

The officers-in-charge/postmasters and their dates in office for the 1970s were **John T. Pope** (June 27, 1973 - Feb. 28, 1976), **James C. Davis, Jr.** (Feb. 28, 1976 - Aug. 14, 1976), **George Vurnakes** (Aug. 14, 1976 - Aug. 6, 1979), and **Edwin H. St. John** (Aug. 6, 1979 - Jan. 26, 1980).

1980s

The Santa Fe Lake Dwellers Association

After Santa Fe Lake residents became alarmed at the threats to the lake in the late 1970s, they formed the Santa Fe Lake Dwellers Association in 1981 under the guidance of **Harold Hill**. Residents were alarmed at efforts by Georgia Pacific to mine the peat from the Santa Fe Swamp. Around that time the Florida Department of Environmental Protection (DEP) named the lake an "Outstanding Florida Water," which makes it, in the words of Section 403.061 (27), Florida Statutes, "worthy of special protection because of [its] natural attributes."

In the end Georgia Pacific donated its swamp holdings to the State of Florida. Now, the Suwannee River Water Management District manages the swamp for hunting and hiking. Members of the Santa Fe Lake Dwellers' Association continue to monitor the water quality of Santa Fe Lake and have earned praise for good stewardship. The many volunteers associated with the association have done a good job in protecting the lake. **Jill McGuire** has been the long-time president of the Santa Fe Lake Dwellers Association.

A t-shirt meant to make local people aware of the problem

LAKEWATCH

Many area residents joined an organization called Florida LAKEWATCH to take monthly samples of the lakes' water to monitor levels of chlorophyll, total phosphorus, and total nitrogen. One of the goals of the area's Lake Dwellers' Association, which many Melrosians also belonged to, was to prevent the extraction of large amounts of peat from the Santa Fe Swamp north of the town.

From 1986 to 1990, **Jean** and **Philip Berkleman** monitored the lakes and collected water samples. From 1990 to the present **Peggy** and **Tom Prevost** have continued with the monitoring.

Representative **Sid Martin**, *who served in the Florida House of Representatives from the mid-1970s through the 1980s, served the area well. Here he is shown presenting a check to the local Homemakers Club in Melrose, perhaps in the 1980s.*

Ordway-Swisher Biological Station

2.7 miles on S.R. 26 east of the traffic light in Melrose at the intersection with S.R. 21 is the Ordway – Swisher Biological Station, run by the Institute of Food and Agricultural Sciences (IFAS) at the University of Florida. The station is a research, teaching, and extension facility meant to study and conserve unique ecosystems.

The entrance to the Ordway-Swisher Biological Station east of Melrose

One part of the facility goes back to **Carl Swisher**, a tobacco industrialist who bought much of the land there from the late 1920s to his death in 1972. For fifty years the tract, which was almost 25,000 acres in size, was the private hunting and fishing preserve of his family and friends.

After Mr. Swisher's death, his family donated around 3,000 acres of the land there to the Nature Conservancy as a memorial to honor him. It became the Carl Swisher Memorial Sanctuary.

In 1980, the Goodhill Foundation, established by **Katharine Ordway** of the 3M Corporation, gave money to the University of Florida Foundation to buy some six thousand acres of pine sandhills from the Swisher Foundation. That land was joined to the Carl Swisher Memorial Sanctuary to become a field station for scientists to learn more about unique ecosystems.

Melrose Public Library, continued

·In 1984 the Melrose Public Library opened (see photo below). In December, 1983, the Boy Scouts had moved seven thousand books from the Scout hut at Trinity Episcopal Church into the new building, which opened on January 22, 1984. The concrete-block building had 3100 square feet of space, enough room for ten thousand books. **Virginia Bird** was the first librarian in the new facility. Branch manager **Stella Brown** succeeded her. (More about the public library in the "2000s" section.)

Problems in Melrose Bay

In 1986, scientists noted a marked increase in total phosphorus levels in Melrose Bay. The scientists blamed the increase on a huge influx of gulls after a strong coastal storm drove the birds inland to the bay. When the gulls left the bay, phosphorus levels returned to normal, but the incident showed how vulnerable local lakes are to outside factors.

The Formation of Historic Melrose, Inc.

In 1985, a group of concerned citizens, led by **Roy Hunt** and **Felicity Trueblood**, formed Historic Melrose, Inc. (HMI) for the purpose of preserving the historic town. It later received a $3,000 state grant from the Division of Historical Resources to conduct an architectural and historic survey of the town and to prepare a nomination packet for the National Register of Historic Places. The first official meeting of Historic Melrose, Inc. took place at the century-old Bonney Farmhouse on April 18, 1988. Over 150 interested people attended the meeting and heard talks by **Roy Hunt**, past president of the Florida Trust for Historic Preservation, and **Vickie Welcher** of the Division of Historical Resources. Eighty new members signed up for HMI at that meeting.

Other important people that first year were **Stephen Lind** (who provided the seed money for a state matching grant that led to a survey of the district), **Zonira Tolles** (who provided much financial assistance to HMI), and **Larry Turner** (who did the articles of incorporation for HMI pro bono).

One of four historic markers in the town is in Heritage Park on S.R. 26.

Traffic light

In 1987, workers installed the town's first traffic light – at the intersection of State Roads 26 and 21. (See photo below.) The traffic light and/or stop signs on S.R. 26 and S.R. 21 caused a lot of confusion when traffic engineers changed them, depending on whether the engineers thought more traffic was using S.R. 26 and therefore ought to have no stop sign or whether they thought that more traffic was using S.R. 21. Motorists were known to miss the newly placed stop sign and shoot through it, sometimes causing traffic accidents. The engineers concluded that a traffic light would be safer and installed it, causing confusion in the first days after installing it.

Postmasters

The Melrose postmasters and their dates in office for the 1980s were **Edwin H. St. John** (Aug. 6, 1979 - Jan. 26, 1980), **William E. Baker** (Jan. 26, 1980 - ??), ??, and **James C. Davis, Jr.** (Feb. 1, 1986 - Jan. 23, 1993). The post office building was built in 1982.

Typical of the very fine restoration work done on old homes in the historic district is the Orr House (pictured to the right). **Nathaniel** and **Elizabeth Orr** (see p. 63+) bought the small board-and-batten house in 1887 and converted it to a comfortable winter cottage they called "Home Acre." When their granddaughter, **Bessie Moore**, who had inherited the house, died, her nephew came down from New York, took the antiques he wanted, and left the rest to the new owner, **Melvin Trent**. Trent's granddaughter occupies the place now.

Melrose Business Association

The Melrose Business Association was formed in 1983 to legally acquire the Melrose Bay beach from the Melrose Junior Woman's Club. The association is committed to improving business relations in the community. They meet monthly. From 1987 to the present, they have sponsored the annual Christmas parade on Bellamy Road in December. They also sponsored a Grape Festival for five years, erected a new Melrose Welcome sign on S.R. 26, and sponsored the July 4th Boat Parade on Santa Fe Lake and recently a Christmas Boat Parade. The group is now known as the Melrose Business and Community Association

People of Melrose

Ms. Mamie Elliott

One of the oldest residents of the Lake Area was Ms. **Mamie Elliott**, who celebrated her ninety-ninth birthday in 1985. She was born in 1886 in Walterburg, South Carolina, and moved to Melrose in 1919, after her husband died.

For over sixty years, she was an active member of the St. Johns Baptist Church, where she was Primary Sunday School teacher for many years and served as the so-called "Mother of the Church" for the young people there. "Aunt Mamie" Elliott was involved in the care of the children and homes of many residents of Melrose.

Cornelius Clayton *(pictured to the left) has been a photographer of many events in Melrose since the 1980s.*

Historic Melrose, Inc. Officers in the 1980s

YEAR	PRESIDENT	VICE-PRES.	SEC.	TREAS.
1988 – 89	E. Williams	M. Watkins	F. Trueblood	D. Melton
1989 – 90	E. Williams	M. Watkins	F. Trueblood	D. Melton

1990s

The National Register of Historic Places

In 1990, a group of concerned citizens, for example **Roy Hunt**, **Felicity Trueblood**, and others, wanted to preserve the best parts of Melrose and petitioned to be on the National Register of Historic Places, which was granted on January 12, 1990. Many of the owners of the historic homes have taken great care in restoring and preserving them for future generations.

Jan and Bill Bolte and the Christmas Bird Count

When **Jan** and **Bill Bolte** (pictured to the right) moved to Melrose from Fort Lauderdale in 1991, they organized the annual Christmas Bird Count and led it for eighteen years. They had conducted the bird count in Fort Lauderdale for 25 years, each served as president of the Broward County Audubon Society, and they were active in the conservation movement there. They also donated a conservation easement on a 142-acre tract to the Land Trust of the Little Tennessee. For twenty years, they also taught nature photography, led nature hikes, and volunteered many hours at the John Campbell Folk School in Brasstown, North Carolina. In 2009 the Santa Fe Audubon Society was organized in Melrose and continues the annual Christmas Bird Count in December.

The 1995 Merry Melrose Christmas Parade

*On December 9, 1995, Historic Melrose, Incorporated
won first place in the category of "closest to theme"
for its float entitled "Melrose at play in an earlier day."*

Historic Melrose, Inc. Officers in the 1990s

YEAR	PRESIDENT	VICE-PRES.	SEC.	TREAS.
1989 – 90	E. Williams	M. Watkins	F. Trueblood	D. Melton
1990 – 91	J. Marshall	Z. Tolles	F. Trueblood	C. Lowry
1991 – 92	R. Daurer	Z. Tolles	F. Trueblood	C. Lowry
1992 – 93	R. Daurer	Z. Tolles	F. Trueblood	C. Lowry
1993 – 94	Z. Tolles	J. Marshall	C. Hutchens	R. Daurer
1994 – 95	Z. Tolles	J. Carr	D. Bartlett	R. Daurer
1995 – 96	J. Carr	A. Vaught	J. Marshall	R. Daurer
1996 – 97	A. Vaught	J. Price	J. Marshall	R. Daurer
1997 – 98	F. Trueblood	Z. Tolles	A. Burt	R. Daurer
1998 – 99	P. Christensen	R. Kash	A. Burt	R. Daurer
1999 – 00	R. Haase	M. O'Brien	A. Burt	R. Daurer

Author/local resident Al Burt

One important member of the community who wrote about Melrose for a large audience throughout the Southeast was **Al Burt** (1927 – 2008). After graduating from the University of Florida (1949), he worked for various newspapers, for example the *Atlanta Journal* and the *Jacksonville Journal* before landing a job with the *Miami Herald*, where he wrote a back-page column for the Sunday magazine about Florida personalities and places. His columns were later collected into three books: *Becalmed in the Mullet Latitudes* (1984), *Al Burt's Florida* (1997), and *Tropic of Cracker* (1999).

In 1965, he was seriously wounded by so-called "friendly fire" while covering the U.S. invasion of the Dominican Republic. He spent the last years of his life in Melrose and then in Jacksonville. In the former he did much to promote the town, for example in supporting the establishment of Heritage Park and in many fund-raising drives.

Local author **Al Burt**
signing
copies of one
of his books
in the public
library in 1997
See the previous page
for more about Al Burt.

A plaque in Melrose's Heritage
Park that honors **Al** *and* **Gloria**
Burt *for their great work in*
supporting the park

When the Florida Legis-
lature passed legislation in 1990 and 2000 to buy more lands for
water-protection and recreation, officials bought many wetlands
and swamps around Lake Alto and the Santa Fe Swamp, although
timbering was still allowed in the Santa Fe Swamp.

Postmasters

The Melrose postmasters and their dates in office for the
1990s were **James C. Davis, Jr.** (Feb. 1, 1986 - Jan. 23, 1993),
Edward A. Teamer (Jan. 23, 1993 - April 30, 1994), and **James
C. Davis, Jr.** (April 30, 1994 - Sept. 19, 2000).

Chapter Five: 21st Century

2000s

Art Galleries

In that decade, a number of artists started coming to town and opening art galleries, three of which still operate. On the first Friday of each month there is an artist's walk that is popular.

Santa Fe Lake

In 2005, workers stocked Santa Fe Lake with 44,500 hybrid-striped bass, after having done so in 1997. Such bass are a hybrid between white bass and striped bass. Other names for the fish are Cherokee bass, palmetto bass, sunshine bass, whiterock bass, and wiper.

A Local Family History

In 2005, **Catherine Price Harmon** and **James "Jimmy" Price** published a history of their family: *The Labon Price Fam-*

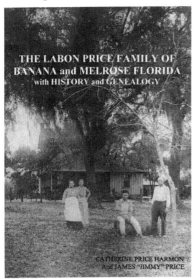

ily of Banana and Melrose, Florida with History and Genealogy, which tells us much about the history of the town and its people.

[Request to other families in Melrose: if anyone else has published a biography of their family that includes a history of the town and surrounding area, please let the co-authors know about this. If there is a second edition of this book, we want to include such books.]

Melrose Heritage Park

In the early 2000s, when developers wanted to build a large store on the land across from Trinity Episcopal Church, concerned citizens joined forces to raise $350,000 to buy the land for what became Heritage Park. It took many fund-raising events to raise that money.

Historic Melrose, Inc. received a grant of $184,000 from the Department of Community Affairs, the Florida Community Trust, and the Florida Forever Program, which enabled them to buy the property in 2001. They paid off the mortgage in 2005.

The first addition to the park was the small building from the M&S (Merchants and Southern) Bank on S.R. 26. That building became the photo museum. When the property mortgage was paid off in full, HMI continued to raise money to build a playground, gazebo, fountain, and lights.

Time Capsule

Local residents placed their Millennium Time Capsule at the Melrose Library on October 7, 2001, containing information and photographs about Melrose in the year 2000.

Sheree Sims, *(on the right) seen here shaking the hand of local resident* **Doris Bartlett**, *helped organize the time-capsule project with the help of many volunteers.*

Paying Off the Mortgage for Heritage Park

In 2003 **Mark Barrow** *(on the left) and* **Terry Marshall** *(on the right) burned the mortgage for the park.*

HMI acquired the Melrose Homemakers Club

In 2002, Historic Melrose, Inc. (HMI) acquired the Melrose Homemakers Club. The white-frame building at the corner of Park and Centre streets, which was built in 1879 as a pharmacy and is located in the historic district, was acquired by the Homemakers in 1950. **Irene Ford**, the current president in 2002 and the only original member of the club still active, and three other club officers signed the deed over to HMI, whose president, **Al Burt**, accepted the property for HMI. The building would become the headquarters for HMI.

The members of the Melrose Homemakers Club that were involved in the transfer of the deed were **Nonie Crom** (vice-president of the Homemakers Club), **Irma Downie** (secretary), and **Mildred Tristani** (treasurer).

Pictured are **Al Burt** *(left, seated),* **Irma Downie** *(left, standing),* **Nonie Crom, Mildred Tristani,** *and* **Irene Ford** *(seated).*

161

Photos from the 2000s

In 2004 auctioneer **Ken Mitchell** *raised $8,800 to help pay off the mortgage for Heritage Park. He also conducted five more auctions to pay for more additions to the park.*

Rosemary Daurer *stands at the door of the Daurer History Center.*

In 2002 the town celebrated the 125th anniversary of the founding of Melrose with a three-day festival and the issuance of a special commemorative stamp.

*One of the local residents who has done much to improve the park is **Joe Rush**, who agreed to fund the installation of permanent restrooms in Heritage Park. He is also in 2017 the president of the Melrose Business Association.*

Yulee Railroad Days

In 2006, Melrose participated in what was called "Yulee Railroad Days" to commemorate the cross-Florida railroad built by Senator **David Levy Yulee** in 1861. Florida's first cross-state railroad went from Fernandina in the northeastern part of the state to Cedar Key on the Gulf of Mexico, but the Civil War put an end to that venture.

A t-shirt commemorated "The Melrose Connection" during the Yulee Railroad Days celebration.

Exhibits were set up in the park to give information about Railroad Days.

HMI board member **Walton Smith** *chaired the Yulee Railroad Days Melrose Connection.*

A Locally Made Quilt

The quilt, which represents the many organizations and businesses in Melrose, is on the interior wall of the headquarters of Historic Melrose, Inc.

Dairy Road Fire

In 2007, a large so-called muck fire, nicknamed the Dairy Road Fire, burned much of the Santa Fe Swamp, both above and below ground, and that led to a huge increase of nutrient concentrations in the three lakes north of Melrose. It was finally put out late that year. The fire had been made worse because the previous seven out of nine years had lower than average rain.

Farmers' Market

On October 7, 2009, the first Farmers' Market was held in Heritage Park. It continues to operate on Fridays under the direction of **Bob Bird** and turned out to be very popular among local residents and visitors.

The Devil's Punch Bowl

The Devil's Punch Bowl (so-called because a youngster drowned there many years ago) is just north of Melrose Bay.

166

Postmasters

The Melrose officers-in-charge/postmasters and their dates in office for the 2000s were **James C. Davis, Jr.** (April 30, 1994 - Sept. 19, 2000), **Linda D. Wheeler** (Sept. 19, 2000 - May 21, 2001), **Gordon "Bud" McInnis** (May 21, 2001 - Aug. 24, 2001), **Danny L. Powers** (Aug. 24, 2001 - Dec. 10, 2001), **David A. Carter** (Dec. 10, 2001 - Jan.. 15 2002), **Melvin F. Wright** (Jan. 15, 2002 - April 20, 2002), **Vicky L. Thompson** (April 20, 2002), ??

Melrose Public Library, continued

As more and more people used the public library, it became apparent that the facility had to expand. The Melrose Library Association took on the task of raising $75,000 for matching state funds to build a children's wing. Local architect **Dore Rotundo**, who had designed the main library building, designed the children's wing. **Edna Williams** donated the land for the library and sold even more land to the association at a nominal price.

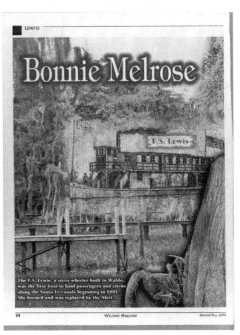

Different regional magazines sometimes featured Melrose in their content, as did this 2004 magazine.

Melrose Public Library, continued

Retired banker **Charles Norton** made a major contribution to the fund-raising, as did Putnam County officials. **Larry Alsobrook** and **Jack Janes** of Breezy Oaks Nursery donated native-plant landscaping. The new building-wing added 1,300 square feet of space, and the book collection of the library as a whole totaled more than twenty-one thousand titles. The grand opening was in May, 2001. **Sheree Sims** became the chief librarian in 2005.

The logo of the children's wing
of the Melrose Library
on the quilt that hangs
in the Homemakers Club

Historic Melrose, Inc. Officers in the 2000s decade

YEAR	PRESIDENT	VICE-PRES.	SEC.	TREAS.
1999 – 00	R. Haase	M. O'Brien	A. Burt	R. Daurer
2000 – 01	P. Christensen	M. O'Brien	G. Ford	S. Sims
2001 – 02	A. Burt	T. Lucas	M. Barrow	S. Sims
2002 – 03	A. Burt	K. Warren	M. Barrow	W. Smith
2003 – 04	M. Barrow	A. Burt	J. Giesel	W. Smith
2004 - 05	M. Barrow	S. Laws	J. Giesel	W. Smith
2005 - 06	S. Laws	M. Barrow	J. Giesel	Barrow/Daurer
2006 - 07	S. Laws	M. Adkins	K. Davis	J. Peffley
2007 - 08	M. Adkins	S. Laws	K. Davis	J. Peffley
2008 - 09	M. Adkins	J. Peffley	K. Davis	M. Barrow
2009 - 10	J. Peffley	M. Adkins	K. Davis	M. Barrow

2010s

In the decade of the 2010s, the long-time drought that dried up some Florida lakes did not adversely affect the lakes in the Santa Fe Lake system, but local residents continued to monitor the lakes, knowing how important those waterways are to the recreational needs of visitors and residents alike.

In 2010, the U.S. Environmental Protection Agency (USEPA) established nutrient criteria for Florida lakes in order to prevent further degradation of water quality and use impairment. That was important for Melrose residents who were determined to protect the bay and Santa Fe lakes. If the lakes had an average chlorophyll concentration above a certain level, officials could classify the lake(s) as eutrophic and possibly take steps to alleviate the situation.

Historic Melrose, Inc. Officers in the 2010s decade

YEAR	PRESIDENT	VICE-PRES.	SEC.	TREAS.
2010 - 11	J. Peffley	J. MacLaren	K. Davis	M. Barrow
2011 - 12	J. MacLaren	J. Peffley	K. Davis	M. Barrow
2012 - 13	J. MacLaren	J. Peffley	K. Davis	M. Barrow
2013 - 14	J. MacLaren	J. Peffley	K. Davis	M. Barrow
2014 - 15	J. Peffley	J. MacLaren	J. Mace	L. Berkleman
2015 - 16	K. Bollum	J. MacLaren	J. Mace	L. Berkleman
2016 - 17	K. Bollum	J. Peffley	K. Bollum	K. Bollum
2017 - 18	K. Bollum	J. Peffley	K.Bollum	Laurel Semmes

In 2011, the Melrose Senior Community Center was built on Bellamy Road. Senior programs, classes, and activities are conducted on Monday, Wednesday, and Friday throughout the year with plans to add more.

Chinese Honeys

Although the terrible freezes of 1894 – 1895 destroyed most of the orange groves in and around Melrose, one type of citrus has made a comeback in the area: Chinese Honeys or Ponkan, a high-yield sweet citrus. The large fruit, once thought to be a pure mandarin, is actually a citrus hybrid of a mandarin and a pumelo. The trees that bear such fruit, which are round and sweet, produce the fruit every year from limbs that can break from heavy yields. Property owners will sometimes prop up the limbs with stakes. Originally introduced into the United States in 1880 by a man named **Carlos Roman**, the fruit has successfully been grown in Hawthorne and Melrose. Melrose has two commercial groves.

The photo here shows co-author **Rosemary Daurer** *at a tree on her property on Melrose Bay. Notice the stick propping up the heavy branch with its Chinese Honeys.*

Conclusion

Melrose can be a busy place for those interested in a variety of activities. Weekly events in the town include dance, music, and art classes at Mossman Hall and a farmers' market in the park. Monthly events include meetings of the Melrose Business and Community Association, the Woman's Club, the Library Association, the Melrose Historic District Committee, Friday Artwalks, concerts at Chiappini's, and the Melrose Dulcimer Group.

A semi-annual event is the Santa Fe Lake Dwellers Association meeting. Also Historic Melrose Inc. has spring and fall tours and an annual meeting in February.

Annual events include a chili cook-off in February to benefit the library, a boat parade on July 4th on Santa Fe Lake, the Melrose Cemetery Association meeting in September, church bazaars in the late fall, a Christmas parade in December, a holiday house tour in December, and a Christmas boat parade on Melrose Bay.

The town has continued to be the home of those who worked elsewhere, for example Gainesville and Palatka, but also for retirees, those with second homes and weekend retreats, and families who wanted to raise their families in safe, pleasant, almost idyllic surroundings.

The town has come a long way from the late nineteenth century when the "Alert" steamed across Melrose Bay on its way to Waldo by way of the Santa Fe Canal.

Appendix 1

Civil War soldiers from the Melrose area -
*indicates a Union soldier

Alderman, Hiram
Buell, Sylvester*
Baldwin, Leonard
Cahoon, James
Clark, Charles
Earle, Elias
Fennell, James
John Fennell
Fickle, Hiram
Ford, Garry
Goodson, Allen
Goodson, Alexander
Grainger, J.F.
Huffman, C.P.*
Jernigan, Levi
Joyner, B.H.
Kelly, David
Labar, James*
Lane, Edmund
Lane, Samuel
Lane, Thomas

Malphurs, James
McLeod, Norman
McRae, Dr. G.W.A.
Merlam, Francis
Moore, Clarence*
Mullen, Nathaniel*
Nobles, Edward
Price, Laban
Reidt, August*
Sherouse, Israel
Stevens, Constant
Suggs, Ezekiel
Suggs, William
Swope, William
Thompson, Thomas
Torlay, S.B.
Ward, Martin L.
Wall, Lawrence
Weeks, R.B.
Weston, Isaac
Wiles, Noah

Appendix 2
Veterans from the Melrose area
who served in World War I

Acosta, Joseph H.
Birt, Harry W.
Chestnut, Bazzle
Daniel, Charles
Danielsen, John
Ford, Frederic H.
Granger, Edmund B.
Huffman, Harry W.
Jackson, Albert
Kelly, Samuel P.

Leggins, Green
Leggins, Willie
Mack, Sidney K.
Mann, Clarence I.
McCartney, Johnson N.
Murphy, Verse
Nobles, Alex
Nobles, Walter
Richardson, Alexander C.
Thomas, Henry

Ware, Jessie

Appendix 3
Veterans from the Melrose area
who served in World War II

A – Army   N – Navy   AF – Air Force   M – Marines
CG – Coast Guard   MM – Merchant Marine □ – Lost their life

Alderman, Eddy A
Alderman, Emory AF
□ Alderman, Harmon N
Alderman, Laurie A
Alderman, Wyman N
Bailey, Jack N
Baker, Anthony MM
Baker, Bruner AF
Baker, Tracy AF
Baker, William MM

Barnett, Hugh A
Barnett, Mary N
Barrington, Herschel N
Beck, Jack A
□ Beck, James N
□ Birsch, Phillip AF
Brantley, Eugene A
Brantley, Warren N
Brantley, Worth A
Bryan, Bobby N

173

Carnes, Eugene A

Chestnut, Morgan A

Chiappini, Francis AF

Chiappini, Maurice A

☐ Clark, Mervin N

Cox, Earl N

Cox, Woodrow N

Cue, Anderson A

Cue, Hilbert A

Daniels, Moses A

☐ Eastmoore, James AF

Eastmoore, Norman AF

Eastmoore, Thomas AF

Flowers, Jimmy A

Ford, R.V. N

Forster, George N

Forster, Henry N

Fox, N

Fox, J.C. M

Fredriksson, Winslow A

French, Curren N

French, Hilyan AF

Gaither, Benny N

Gaither, William AF

Gornto, Dan N

Grainger, Adell A

Grainger, Frank N

Greathouse, Brady N

Hill, Harold CG

Hogan, E.F. CG

Hogan, Harold CG

Holmes, George

Johnson, Charles N

Johnson, Edgar N

Johnson, Floyd N

Jordan, Roy N

Kite, Murphey N

Martin, A.D. A

Matchett, Grover M

Melvin, Gerald N

Mills, Arthur A

Mills, David A

Morris, Howard A

Murray, Alex CG

Neilson, Paul N

Nobles, Harold N

Nobles, Russell A

Perry, Clarence N

Preston, Harold N

Price, Allen N

Price, Charles A

Price, Herman A

Price, Jimmy N

Ridaught, Harold A

Ridaught, Hubert AF

Ridaught, Leon M

Roberson, Bill N

Robinson, Elwyn N

Robinson, Wynell A

Robinson, Harold N

☐ Robinson, Rexall A

Roundtree, Bill AF

Roundtree, Bob N

Rountree, Crosley M

Rountree, Emery A

Rountree, T.C. N

Seigler, Donald N
Seigler, Maurice AF
Shipman, Bobby N
Sikes, H.B. N
Sikes, Jimmy A
Stewart, Pete N
Strickland, Ben N
Strickland, Bobby A
Strickland, Clyde A
Strickland, Harry AF
☐ Tanner, Donald A
Terrell, Corbett N
Terrell, Leroy N
Thomas, Vernie AF

Tillis, Alton A
Tison, Dock N
Tison, Lawrence N
Turner, Adolphus N
Tyre, Hazel N
Tyre, Irving A
Tyre, Paul AF
Tyre, Roy A
Vaught, Alfred A
Walters, Frank AF
Ward, Sidney N
Watts, Thomas N
Weeks, J.C. N
Whitney, Andrew MM

Yarbrough, Elmo A

The co-authors wish to send a special thank-you to veteran **Jimmy Price** for his great effort in compiling the list of all the Melrose veterans. We have tried to collect the names of those Melrose veterans who fought in the Korean, Vietnam, and Iraq-Afghanistan wars, but more recent privacy laws have not allowed us to do so. If we have left out any names of veterans in the three wars listed, please let one of the co-authors know, and we will correct the lists if there is a second edition.

A monument to those who served their country in the Armed Forces was erected at the entrance to the Melrose Cemetery in May, 2007.

Scenes Around Melrose in 2017

The gymnasium at the school in 2016.

The Ameris Bank, formerly the F.W. Tolles House

A local well-known restaurant: Blue Water Bay

The popular Melrose Café

A local gift shop and gallery: Artisans Way Silver Linings

Gallery 26 Art Gallery

Melrose Bay Art Gallery

In 2017, three descendants of pioneer families in Melrose posed for a photo at HMI's annual meeting – from left to right: **John McRae, Jimmy Price,** *and* **Harry Jackson II.**

179

About the Authors

Rosemary Baxa was born in 1928 in Chicago and went to Northern Illinois State Teachers' College (now Northern Illinois University). She graduated from there in 1950 with a major in Physical Education and a minor in Health Education before teaching for two years near Chicago. She later worked at Chicago's Museum of Science and Industry, where she was a lecturer in Biology and Physics. While working for a master's degree in Physical Education at Northwestern University, she taught in Dekalb, Illinois. There she met **Joe Daurer** and married him in 1956. They moved to Memphis, TN, and then Keystone Heights, FL, where she worked as secretary for the Chamber of Commerce. She and Joe moved to Melrose in 1961. She has been there ever since. She earned a master's degree (M.P.E.H.) at the University of Florida in 1966 and taught there from 1966 until 1973. Joe, a combat photographer in World War II, became more involved in photography when he retired. The Daurers collected old photos of the area, annotated them, and improved them.

Kevin McCarthy, who was born in 1940, earned his B.A. in American Literature from LaSalle College (1963), his M.A. in English from the University of North Carolina – Chapel Hill (1966) and his Ph.D. in Linguistics from the same school (1970). He taught in the Peace Corps in Turkey for two years, in Lebanon as a Fulbright Professor for one year, in Saudi Arabia as a Fulbright Professor for two years, and as a professor of English and Linguistics at the University of Florida for 33 years. He has had 66 books published, mostly about Florida, plus several dozen articles in scholarly and popular journals and has given over 300 talks to schools and academic groups. In 2003 the University of Florida named him its Distinguished Alumni Professor. Since retiring from the University of Florida in 2005, he has taught writing workshops in Hanoi, Vietnam two times, and has taught English-as-a-Foreign Language in Spain four times. He continues to research and write nonfiction books.

Bibliography

Burt, Al. "Melrose - A Reflection of Florida's Past," *Florida Trend*, vol. 44, no. 10 (January 2002), p. S12.

Burt, Al. "Melrose," *Florida Monthly*, January, 2002, pp. 6-9.

Canfield Jr., Daniel E. and others, "Water quality changes at an Outstanding Florida Water: influence of stochastic events and climate variability," *Lake and Reservoir Management*, vol. 32, no. 3 (2016), pp. 297 - 313.

Eschbach, Philip, "Melrose, Florida has a long and colorful history," *Florida Postal History Society Journal*, vol. 20, no. 3 (September, 2013), pp. 13 – 17.

Ferm, Lois, "Billy Graham in Florida," *Florida Historical Quarterly*, vol. 60, no. 2 (October, 1981), pp. 174 – 185.

Fronabarger, Nell McRae and Ray E. Fronabarger. *Christopher & Catherine McRae*. Greenville, SC: Southern Historical Press, Inc., 1997

Harmon, Catherine Price and James "Jimmy" Price. *The Labon Price Family of Banana and Melrose, Florida with History and Genealogy*. Melrose?: Catherine Price Harmon, 2005.

Howard, Kennie L. *Yesterday in Florida*. New York: Carlton Press, Inc., 1970.

Meyer, Jessie Hamm. *Leading the Way: A Century of Service – The Florida Federation of Women's Clubs, 1895 – 1995*. Lakeland, FL: GFWC Florida Federation of Women's Clubs, Inc., 1994.

Michaels, Brian E. and the Putnam County Action '76 Heritage Task Force Historical Manuscript Subcommittee. *The River Flows North: A History of Putnam County, Florida*. Palatka, FL: Putnam County Archives and History Commission, 1986.

Morris, Allen. *Florida Place Names*. Sarasota, FL: Pineapple Press, Inc., 1995.

Perkins, Virginia, "Melrose: The Bonnie Town by the Bay," *Country Chronicle*, January 1997, p. 3.

Pinckney, Paul, "Lesson Learned from the Charleston Quake: How the Southern City Was Rebuilt Finer Than Ever within Four Years, *San Francisco Chronicle*, May 6, 1906; internet site: http://www.sfmuseum.org/1906.2/charleston.html.

Ruiz-Bernard, Ivelisse. "Effects of a catastrophic forest fire on strophic parameters of an outstanding Florida water system." M.S. Thesis, University of Florida, 2012.

Tolles, Zonira Hunter. *Bonnie Melrose: The Early History of Melrose, Florida*. Gainesville: Storter Printing Co., 1982.

Tolles, Zonira Hunter. *Shadows on the Sand: A History of the Land and the People in the Vicinity of Melrose, Florida*. Keystone Heights, FL: Tolles, 1976 - Storter Printing Co.

Von Noszky, H. "An Indian Battlefield near Melrose," *Florida Historical Quarterly*, vol. 2, no. 1 (April, 1909), pp. 47 - 48.

Watkins, Caroline, "Some Early Railroads in Alachua County." *Florida Historical Quarterly*, 53 (4) (April 1975): pp. 450–59

Webber, "Carl." *The Eden of the South, descriptive of the orange groves, vegetable farms, strawberry fields, peach orchards, soil, climate, natural peculiarities, and the people of Alachua County, Florida*. New York: Leve & Alden, 1883.

Photo credits

Unless otherwise noted, the individual photographs were supplied by **Rosemary Daurer** from the **Joe** and **Rosemary Daurer** Collection. Other credits refer to the pages on which the photographs occur.

Kevin McCarthy: title page, page opposite p. 1, pp. 1, 2,14 15,16 (both), 17 (bottom), 19, 20 (both), 21, 23 (bottom), 25, 35 (both), 38, 46,54, 94 (bottom), 101 (bottom), 109 (bottom), 111, 113 (bottom), 114, 116 (both), 120 (bottom), 122, 125, 142, 144, 145, 146, 147, 155 (bottom), 157 (bottom), 158, 162 (bottom), 166 (bottom),170, 175, 176 (both), 177 (both), 178 (both), 179 (both).

State Archives of Florida, Florida Memory: pp. 5,6,9,10,12,13,24,26, 27,28,31,33 (top), 36, 68, 103 (both).

Keith McInnis: cover photo of a painting by Justin Pearson, a painting housed in the Matheson History Museum, which gave us permission to use the image; also p. 171.

Matthew McCarthy: p. 3 from the Florida Department of Environmental Protection.

Marshall, Jean - Historic Melrose Inc. photos, 1989 - 2017

Matheson History Museum: p. 4.

Internet: pp. 7 (Ebyabe), 39 (bottom), 51 (bottom), 92 (both), 156.

Smithsonian American Art Museum: p. 11.

Wikipedia: p. 49

English Wikipedia: p. 39 (top).

University of Florida Archives: p. 51 (top).

Library of Congress: pp. 64, 111.

Clay County Archives: pp. 86, 87.

INDEX

3M Corporation, 148
Acosta, Joseph, 173
Adkins, M.., 168
Adventists, 6
Af.-Americans, 89
Al Burt's Florida, 156
Alachua County, 1,10, 24,25,29,30,44,49,50, 74,86,120,152
Alaska, 5
Albany County, NY, 63
Albany, NY, 18,63
Alderman, Eddy, 173
Alderman, Emory, 173
Alderman, H., 86
Alderman, Harmon, 173
Alderman, Hiram, 172
Alderman, Laurie, 173
Alderman, Sarah, 108
Alderman, Wyman, 173
"Alert," 28-30,32,171 (boat)
Alex Craig Store, 81
Allen, Jean, 126
Alsobrook, Larry, 168
Am. Assoc. of Retired Persons, 136
American Civil War, 14-16,22,24,36,89,164
Am. Revolution, 36
Ameris Bank, 176
Apalachee, 6
Archer, FL, 14
Armed Forces, 175
Armed Occupation Act, 12

Art galleries, 158
Artisans Way Silver Linings, 178
Atlanta Journal, 156
Atlantic, Gulf & West India Transit Co., 24
Aycock, Virginia, 105

Bachman, Gwen, 143
Bailey, Jack, 173
Bailey, Mr., 44
Baker, Anthony, 173
Baker, Bruner, 173
Baker, Tracy, 173
Baker, William, 151, 173
Baldwin, FL,14
Baldwin Store, 94, 102
Baldwin, Emma, 83
Baldwin, L.M., 83,84
Baldwin, Leonard, 172
Banana (community), 15,18-22,31,45
Banana Burying Ground, 15
Banana Post Office, 18,20,26
Baptist Church, 113
Barnett, Hugh, 173
Barbot, Grace, 137
Barnett, J.M., 86
Barnett, James, 45

Barnett, Mary, 173
Barnett, May, 83
Barrington, Herschel, 173
Barrow, Mark, 160, 168,169
Bartlett, D., 155
Bartlett, Doris, 160
Bay Street, 84
Bayview, 37,41,56, 105,127,141
Becalmed in the Mullet Latitudes, 156
Beck, Jack, 173
Beck, James, 173
Bellamy Avenue, 107
Bellamy Road, 10,15, 37,45,59,60,85,95, 98,100,106,125,126
Bellamy, John, 10
Belle Heiress, The, 63
Benson, David, 137
Benson, Jo, 137
Bering Strait, 5
Beringia, 5
Berkleman, Jean, 147
Berkleman, Phil, 147
Berkleman, L., 169
Best Beard Contest, 131
Betsy Ross float, 132
Bird, Bob, 166
Bird, Virginia, 149
Birsch, Phillip, 173
Birt, Harry, 173
Blue Water Bay Restaurant, 62,177
Board of Public Instruction, 122
Board, J.A., 84
Boat parades, 170
Bolden, Jerry, 134

184

Bollum, Keith, 169
Bolte, Bill, 154
Bolte, Jan, 154
Bonney Farm, 22,150
Bonney Place, 22
Bonney, C.D., 22
Bonney, William, 22
Bonnie Melrose, 18, 141
Bonnie Melrose, 167 (magazine)
Bonnie Mount, 22,23
Bonnie View, 22
Boston, GA, 114
Bostwick, FL, 115
Boy Scouts, 111,123, 125,126,142,147,149
Bradford County, 1,4, 30,44,49
Brantley, Eugene, 173
Brantley, Warren, 173
Brantley, Worth, 173
Brasstown, NC, 154
Breezy Oaks Nursery, 168
Brinson, Emma, 91
Broward County Audubon Soc., 154
Brown Family, 89
Brown, Mr., 112
Brown, Stella, 149
Brownies, 125
Bryan, Bobby, 173
Buell, Sylvester, 172
Burial Mounds, 7,8
Burt, Al, 155-57, 161,168
Burt, Gloria, 157

Cahoon, James, 172
Callahan, FL, 14
Calusa, 6
Camp Blanding, 121
Canal Transportation Co., 36
Carl Swisher Mem. Sanct., 148
Carnes, Eugene, 174
Carpenter Gothic-style, 46
Carr, J., 155
Carter, David, 167
Cattle muzzles, 51
Cedar Key, FL, 14,24, 27,164
Centre Street, 59,75, 161
Charleston Earthquake of 1886, 49
Charleston, SC, 49
Chatham, CT, 52
Cherokee bass, 158
Chestnut, Bazzle, 173
Chestnut, Morgan, 174
Chiappini, "Papa Joe," 112
Chiappini, Francis, 174
Chiappini, Maurice, 174
Chiappini's Gas Station, 112,170
Chinese honeys, 170
Christensen, P., 155
Christmas Bird Count, 154

Christmas parade, 152,171
Cimarrón, 9
"City of Melrose," 105 (boat)
Civil War (see American Civil War)
Civil War memorial, 16
Clark, Charles, 172
Clark, Mervin, 174
Clay County, FL, 1,4,30,44,4,30,44, 49,74,86,87,108
Clayton, Cornelius, 153
Confederate soldiers, 15,16,39
Congress, 12
Cooper, Edna, 99
Cotton gins, 48
Coward, Mr., 81
Coward, Simon, 81,84
Coward, Stella, 83
Cox, Earl, 174
Cox, Woodrow, 174
Craig, Alex, 81
Craig, A.W., 84
Craig, William, 38,45,84
Crom, Nonie, 161
Crosby, Mary, 103
Cross-Florida railroad, 164
Crystal River St. Arch. Site, 7
Crystal River, FL, 7
Cue, Anderson, 174
Cue, Hilbert, 174
Cypress Street, 59,60,106

Dairy Road Fire, 165

Dampier, Thelma, 142

Dampier, Rudolph, 142

Daniel, Charles, 173

Daniels, Moses, 174

Danielsen, John, 173

Daurer History Center, 162

Daurer, Joe, 137,138, 176,180

Daurer, Rosemary, 16,55,158,162, 170,180

Davis Railroad Depot, 101

Davis, James, 151

Davis, Jr., James, 145,157,167

Davis, K., 169

De Bry, Theodorus, 6

De León, Juan Ponce, 6

De Soto, Hernando, 11

Dept. of Community Affairs, 159

Devil's Punch Bowl/ Lake, 89,166

Devonia Street, 109

Div. of Hist. Resources, 150

Div. of Historical Resources, 150

"Dixie," 77 (boat)

Dominican Republic, 156

Downie, Irma, 161

Drayton Island, FL, 7

Dulcimer group, 170

Dunbar, Elmer, 81

Dunbar, Mr., 112

Dunbar, Wilbur, 81

Earle, Elias, 172

Earleton, FL, 28

East Florida, 10

Easter season, 6

Eastmoore, James, 174

Eastmoore, Norman, 174

Eastmoore, Thomas, 174

Eden of the South, 25-27

Edwards, Mr., 112

Eliam Baptist Church, 15, 17,18, 22,43,104,122

Elliott, Mamie 153

England, 65,91

English Madrigal Dinners, 136,137

Episcopal Boy Scout House, 122

Etoniah Creek, 8,18, 19

Etoniah Stream Dredge & Canal Co., 22

Europeans, 9

Everglades, 11

Ewing, Robert, 36

"F.S. Lewis," 27,29 (boat)

F.W. Tolles House, 176

Faikel, Mabel, 143

Faith Presbyterian Church, 136

Farmers' Markets, 166

Farrell, Ned, 26,30

Fennell, James, 172

Ferm, Lois, 106,115

Fernandina – Cedar Key Railroad, 26

Fernandina, FL, 14,24,27,164

Fickle, Hiram, 68,172

Fire Dept. – see Melrose Fire Dept.

Fire-fighting, 119,120

Fl. Central & Pen. Railroad Co., 69

Fl. Community Trust, 159

Fl. Dept. of Env. Protection, 146

Fl. Fed. of Women Clubs, 66

Fl. Federation of Women's Clubs, 123

Fl. Fish & Wildlife Cons. Com., 3

Fl. Forever Program, 159

Fl. General Assembly, 14

Fl. Historical Quarterly, 11,106,115

Fl. Historical Society, 128

Fl. House of Rep., 147

Fl. Legislature, 145,157

FL. Senators, 14

Fl. Statutes, 146

Fl. Trust for Hist. Preservation, 150

Float, Marguerita, 128

Florida LAKE-WATCH, see LAKE-WATCH

Florida Place Names, 34

Florida Railroad, 24

Florida State, 171

Flowers, Jimmy, 174

Ford, Fred, 84

Ford, Frederic, 173

Ford, Garry, 172

Ford, Irene, 161

Ford, R.V., 174

Forster, George, 174

Forster, Henry, 174

Forster, Mr., 112

Fort Lauderdale, FL, 154

Fox, Everett, 174

Fox, J.C., 174

Fox, Lucy, 45,68

Fredriksson, Winslow, 174

Freedmen, 15

French, Curren, 174

French, Hilyan, 174

Friday Artwalks, 170

Front Street, 116

Gainesville, FL, 1, 2, 8,14,24,59,93,116, 117,171

Gaither, Benny, 174

Gaither, William, 174

Gallery 26 Art Gallery, 178

Geneva, FL, 30

Georgia Pacific, 146

Giesel, J., 168

Gilmore, George, 91

Gilmore, Rev., 59

Girl Scout Troup 418, 131

Goodhill Foundation, 148

Goodson, Alexander, 30,38,86,172

Goodson, Allen, 172

Goodson, M.C., 38

Goodson, Ruth, 94

Gornto, Dan, 174

Graham, Billy, 106,115

Grainger, Adell, 174

Grainger, Frank, 174

Grainger, J.F. , 172

Granger, Edmund, 173

Granger, Meredith, 30

Great Depression, 66

Great Hall of Trinity Epis. Church, 134

Greathouse, Brady, 174

Green Cove Springs & Melrose Railroad, 55,67

Green Cove Springs, 55,67,68

Green Street, 116

Green, C.S., 114

Greenbury, 38

Grove Street, 55,107,116,123

Gulf coast, 12

Gulf of Mexico, 3, 164

Haase, Ron, 155, 168,168

Hagan, Benjamin, 103

Hagan, Napoleon, 103

Hall, John, 63

Hamlyn, Effie, 64

Hamlyn, Mrs. Walter, 99,109

Hamlyn, Walter, 64, 99,109,112

Hamlyn's property, 59,112

Hampton Street, 42,45,81,100,126

Hancock, Sheriff, 114

Harmon, Catherine, 158

Harned, Mr., 112

Harper, Annie, 107

Hawkins, Mr., 86

Hawthorne Reporter, 128

Hawthorne, FL, 143,170

"Here Today, Here Tomorrow," 144

Heritage Park, 2,6, 101,106,124,150, 156-59,163,164,166

Highway 1471, 25

Hill, C.C., 86
Hill, Harold, 146,174
Hilton, John, 84
Hist. of the M. Public Library, 91,111,123
Historic Melrose, Inc., 19,51,62,123, 150,155,159,161,164,165,168,170
History museums, 169
Hogan, E.F., 174
Hogan, Harold, 174
Hohokus, NJ, 64
Hollis, Bob, 133
Hollis, Ruth 133
Holmes, Elizabeth, 63
Holmes, George, 174
"Home Acre," 63,152
Homemakers Club, 62,111, 123,147, 161,168
Homes Family, 89
Hotel Santa Fe, 75
Howard, Kennie, 8, 38,40,41,47,49,50, 58,59,67,89,104,109,118
Huffman, C.P., 84,172
Huffman, Charlie, 142

Huffman, Harry, 120,142,169,173
Huffman, Nettie, 83
Hulett, Olive, 126
Hunt, Roy, 150,154
Husband Brothers, 109
Husband, Neva, 90
Husband, Orville, 47,98,100, 104,109, 112
Husband, Sara, 98
Hutchens R., 155
Hutchings, Bill, 99
Hutchings, Mrs., 99

IFAS, 148
Improvement Society, 66
"Indian Princess," 77,78,99 (boat)
Indian Territory, 11
Ingram, Mrs. O.R., 114
Inst. of Food and Agric. Sciences, 148
Internal Improvement Act, 14
Internat. Tennis Hall of Fame, 64
Iowa, 13
Iraq-Afghanistan War Veterans, 175
Italy, 112

Jackson House, 38
Jackson, Albert, 173

Jackson, Greenberry, 38,94
Jackson, Harriett, 94
Jackson, Harry, 94-96
Jackson, H., 84
Jackson II, Harry, 38, 179
Jacksonville Police Dept., 103
Jacksonville, FL, 1,15,26,29,103,156
Jacksonville, Journal, 156
Janes, Jack, 137,168
Jernigan, Levi, 172
John Campbell Folk School, 154
John Fennell, 172
Johnson, Charles, 174
Johnson, Edgar, 174
Johnson, Floyd, 174
Jordan, Roy, 174
Joyner, B.H., 172
Judd, E.L., 59,65
Judd, Edson, 46
Jumonville, PA, 56

Kash, R., 155
Kater, Oonagh, 137
Keener Family, 127
Keener, Russell, 127
Kelly, David, 172
Kelly, Samuel, 173
Kentucky, 23
King, Eliza, 65
King, W.W., 105
King, Zella, 105
Kirkland Family, 89
Kite, Murphey, 174

Korean War Veterans, 175

Lake Alto, 3,4,26,157
Labar, James, 172
Lake Geneva, 30
Lake Rosa, 11
Lake Swan, 106,115
LAKEWATCH, 144, 147
Lambdin, Ella, 37,97
Lambdin, McKendrie, 23,29,36,37, 40,50,58,89,97
Lambdins, 23,37,41,56,97
Land Trust of the Little Tennessee, 154
Lane, Edmund, 172
Lane, Samuel, 172
Lane, Thomas, 172
Latchstring House, 78,79
Latchstring Road, 78
Laudonnière, René, 6
Laws, S., 168
Le Moyne, Jacques, 6
Leading the Way, 66
Lee Family, 36, 108, 114
Lee House, 36, 114, 121
Lee sisters, 90
Lee, Addie, 114
Lee, Alice, 108
Lee, Anna, 114
Lee, Homer, 114
Lee, John, 114
Lee, Paul, 60,108,114
Lee, Robert, 114
Lee, W.H., 84

Lee, William, 60, 108
Leggins, Green, 173
Leggins, Willie, 173
Lewis Family, 89
Lewis Plantation, 35
Lincoln Ford Car Dealership, 106,142
Lind, Stephen, 150
Lit. and Debating Society, 65, 66,91, 125,126,145
Little Santa Fe Lake, 3,4,99,144
Loch Katrina, 39
London, Ontario 63
Looney, G.C., 87
Looney, George, 44,75,76
Louisville, KY, 86
Love, Mr., 112
Lower Creek Indians, 9
Lowry, C., 155
Lucas, T., 168
Lunsden, Olive, 112
Lutheran ministers, 56
Lutherans, 91
Lynch, G. M., 87
Lynn, Joseph, 86
Lyons, Cara , 83

M&S Bank, 159
MacDonald, Martha, 89
Mack, Sidney, 173
Mack, V.L., 84
MacLaren, J., 169
Malphurs, James, 172
Mann, Clarence, 173

Mann, Walter, 126, 142
Marion County, FL, 105
Marshall, Jean, 155
Marshall, Terry, 160
Martin, A.D., 174
Martin, Sid, 143,147
Masonic fraternity, 87
Matchett, Grover, 174
Matthews, Ralph, 119
McCarthy, Kevin, 180
McCartney, Johnson, 173
McGee, Mary, 127, 128
McGregor, A.G., 84
McGuire, Jill, 146
McInnis, Gordon, 167
McLeod, John, 56
McLeod, Norman, 172
McRae Store, 58
McRae, "Wash," 86
McRae, A.A., 58, 84,96
McRae, Claudia, 62, 83
McRae, Dr. G.W.A., 172
McRae, Frank, 15,18, 62,84,86,96
McRae, George, 18, 20,22
McRae, John, 86,179
McRae's Drugstore, 123
Melrose Abbey, 39

189

Melrose Academy, 86,87

Melrose Action Committee, 129

Melrose Arts & Crafts Festivals, 129

Melrose Bay, 1,3,4,22, 23,37,52,63,78,104,121, 127,144,149,166,171, 179

Melrose Bay Art Gallery, 179

Melrose Beach, 127, 152

Melrose Bowlers, 112

Melrose Bus. Assoc., 152,163

Melrose Business Assoc., Inc., 129,170

Melrose Café, 177

Melrose Cemetery, 14,15,42,171,175

Melrose Centennial Celebration, 130-35, 138-42

Melrose Community School, 129

Melrose Elem. School, 145

Melrose Fire Dept., 117,118,128,130

Melrose Homemakers Club (see Homemakers Club

Melrose Inn, 37,44, 75,78,80,88,142

Melrose Jail, 93

Melrose Judo Club, 129

Melrose Jun. Woman's Club, 125, 152

Melrose Library Assoc., 167,170

Melrose Lutheran Church, 107

Melrose Negro School No. 4, 87

Melrose Public Library, 91,111,121, 124,145,149,157,16 7,168

Melrose Railroad Station, 67

Melrose School, 126

Melrose Sen. Com. Center 169

Melrose Woman's Club, 74,105,122,12 5,126,135,136,143,1 45,170

Melrose, Scotland, 39

Melton, D., 153,155

Melvin, Gerald, 174

Merchants and Southern Bank, 159

Merlam, Francis, 172

Merlin the Magician, 137

Merry Melrose Parade, 155

Methodist Church, 93,122

Methodist Episcopal Church, 42

Meyer, Jessie, 66

Miami Herald, 156

Miami, FL,59,117, 118

Michaels, Brian, 20

Milanich, Jerald, 6

Mills, Arthur, 174

Miller, Dewitt, 92

Mills, David, 174

Minder, John,106,117

Mission Chapel, 56

Mississippi, 36

Mississippi River, 36

Mitchell, Ken, 162

Mizell, Kate, 83

Mobile, AL, 114

Mollas, Frank, 68

Moore, Bessie, 152

Moore, Clarence, 172

Moore, Elisabeth, 63

Moore, Sarah, 64

Morris, Allen, 34

Morris, Flora, 83

Morris, Howard, 174

Morrison Store, 81

Mosely, J.J., 39

Mosely, William, 39

Mossman, Mary, 107

Mossman Hall, 107,170

Mount Royal, 7

Mrs. Lee's millinery shop, 60

Mullen, Margaret, 85

Mullen, Nathaniel, 85, 68,172

Mullen, Sadie, 85

Mullin (or Mullen), Sadie, 83

Murphy, Verse, 173

Murray, Alex, 174

Nat. Law Enforcement Mem., 103

Native Americans, 5-12

Nature Conservancy, 148

Neale, Bobby, 137

Neale, Elisa, 137
Neale, Elizabeth, 137
Neale, Jimmy, 137
Nebraska, 83
Neilson, Paul, 174
New Jersey, 107
New World, 9
New York City, NY
63,112
New York State, 171
No. 11 Lake, 30
Nobles, Alex, 102,173
Nobles, Charles, 84
Nobles, Edward, 172
Nobles, Harold, 174
Nobles, Russell, 174
Nobles, Walter, 173
North America, 5
North Florida, 6,7
North, 15,48,57
North-central Florida,
5,12,14
Northeast Florida, 6
Northwestern Florida,
6
Norton, Charles, 168
Nutmeg house, 52

O'Brien, M., 155
Oberry, Miss, 44
Ocala, FL, 24
Octagon-style houses,
52
Ohio, 38
Orange Heights, 94-96
Orange Springs Road,
8
Ordway, Katharine,
148
Ordway-Swisher Bio-
logical Sta., 148

Orr Family,
63,64,152
Orr House, 152
Orr, Elisabeth, 152
Orr, Nathaniel, 63,
152
Osceola, 11
Outstanding Florida
Water, 146

Painter, A.P., 45
Palatka, FL, 1,2 7,15,
62,114, 115,171
Paleoindians, 5
Palmetto bass, 158
Park Avenue, 38,43
Park Street, 60,75,
81,161
Pass, 4
Patents, 51,92
Payne, John, 68
Pearl Street, 42,107
Pearsall Circle, 77
Pearsall, Alfred, 77-
79,96
Pearsall, Clifford, 77
Pearsall, Edna, 77
Pearsall, Grace, 77
Pearsall, Harriet, 99
Pearsall, J. Herbert,
77
Pearsall, Leigh, 8,77,
78,82,88,89,99,
109,112
Pearsall, Morgan, 101
Pearsall, Mrs. Leigh,
99
Pearsall, Ralph, 77
Pearsall, Robert, 101
Pearsall, Ruth, 77
Peffley, J., 168,169

Pelham Family, 89
Pensacola, FL, 10
Perkins, Virginia, 39
Perry, Clarence, 174
Phi Sigma College,
75,76
Philadelphia, PA, 40
Phillips, Mattie, 103
Phillips, T.J. , 42
Pilcher Family, 89
Pinckney, Paul, 49
Pine Street, 44,55,
56,75
Platform mounds, 7
Plymouth County,
MA, 105
Ponkan, 170
Pope, John, 145
Postmasters, 38,45,6
8,85,112,127,128,14
3,149,155,163
Potter, Mr., 112
Powers, Danny, 167
Pre-Columbian Nat.
Americans, 7
Preston, Harold, 174
Prevost, Peggy, 147
Prevost, Tom, 147
Price, Allen, 174
Price, Charles, 174
Price, Herman, 174
Price, J., 155
Price, James, 158,
174,175,179
Price, Laban, 172
Priest, Eva, 83
Priest, N.E., 84
Priolrau, Jr., Philip,
51
Public libraries,
56,66
Pumelos, 170
191

Punch Bowl – see Devil's Punch Bowl
Punch Bowl Lake, 89
Putnam County, FL, 1,4,20,30,44,49,54, 74,106,110,126, 145,168

Quail Street, 37,41, 52,56,74,104

Reconstruction, 15
Reid, 58
Reidt, August, 172
Richardson, Alexander, 173
Ridaught, Harold, 174
Ridaught, Hubert, 174
Ridaught, Leon, 174
Roberson, Bill, 174
Robinson Store, 58
Robinson, El, 105
Robinson, Elwyn, 174
Robinson, Harold, 174
Robinson, Rexall, 174
Robinson, Wynell, 174
Roman, Carlos, 170
Rood, Ray, 137
Rosewood (house), 65
Rotundo, Dore, 167
Roundtree, Bill, 174
Roundtree, Bob, 174

Rountree, Crosley, 174
Rountree, Emery, 174
Rountree, T.C., 174
Rush, Joe, 163

S.R. 21, 4,21,22,44, 112,151,152
S.R. 26,10,16,55,74, 95,98,112,125,126, 150,151,159
"Sanitary Town of Florida," 69
Santa Fe Audubon Soc., 154
Santa Fe Canal Co., 26,171
Santa Fe Hotel, 55
Santa Fe Lake Dwellers Assn., 144, 146,147,170
Santa Fe Lake, 1,3,4, 8,26-28,30,36,57,77, 144,146,158,171
Santa Fe Lake System, 169,171
Santa Fe River, 3
Santa Fe Swamp Wild. & Env. Area, 3
Santa Fe Swamp, 3,146,147,157,165
Sawmills, 36,43,47, 57,61,89
Scotland, 39
Scott, Mr., 44
Scott, Walter, 39
Second Seminole War, 12
Seigler, Donald, 175

Seigler, Maurice, 175
Seminary Ridge Road, 22
Seminole Indian Wars, 12,14
Seminoles, 9,11
Semmes, Laurel, 169
Sexton, Dowing, 52
Shadows on the Sand, 138,141
Shakerag, 34,130,140
Sheats, W.N., 86
Shell mounds, 7
Sherouse, Israel, 172
Shipman, Bobby, 175
Sikes, H.B., 175
Sikes, Jimmy, 175
Sims, Sheree, 160, 168
Sims, William, 30
Sipprell, Murray, 136
Slaves, 13,15,89
Smith, Walton, 164,168
Soc. for the Prop. of Christian Knowledge, 91
South Florida, 129
South Georgia, 9
South Street, 95,101
Southeast, 49,156
Spaniards, 9
Spanish army, 9
Spires, Mildred, 126
St. Augustine, FL, 9,10w
St. John, Edwin, 145,151
St. Johns Baptist Church, 153
St. Johns River, 6,7, 12,67

St. Luke's Lutheran
Church, 56
State of Florida, 146
Stevens, Betty, 152
Stevens, Billy, 152
Stevens, Constant,
172
Stewart, Frank,
112,121,127
Stewart, Pete, 175
Stokes; Laurie, 83
Strickland, Ben, 175
Strickland, Bobby,
175
Strickland, Clyde,
175
Strickland, Harry,
175
Sugar cane, 58,59
Suggs, Ezekiel, 172
Suggs, William, 172
Sunshine bass, 158
Suw. River Water
Management Dis.,
146
Suwannee Riv. Wat.
Man., 3
Suwannee River, 3
Swisher Foundation,
148
Swisher, Carl, 148
Swope, William, 172

Tallahassee, FL,
5,10,50
Tampa – Jacksonville
Railroad, 55
Tampa, FL, 55,115
Tanner, Donald, 175
Teamer, Edward, 157
Temple Mounds, 8

TenEyk, 135
TenEyk, Lynn, 135,
137
TenEyk, Martha, 135
Terrell, Corbett, 175
Terrell, Leroy, 175
"The Hall," 65,66, 145
*The Labon Price Family
of Banana and Melrose,*
158
Thomas, Henry, 173
Thomas, Vernie, 175
Thompson, Thomas,
172
Thompson, Vicky, 167
Tillis, Alton, 175
Time capsules, 160
Timucua, 6
Tison, Dock, 175
Tison, Lawrence, 175
Tolles, Zonira, 18,138,
141,150,155
Torlay, S.B., 172
Town Square, 100
Treadwell, Alice, 99
Tredwell, Alice, 64
Trent, Melvin, 152
Trinity Episcopal
Church, 46,59,60,91,
111,123,126,136,
149,159
Tristani, Mildred, 161
Tropic of Cracker,
156
Trout Street, 9,32,37,
38,43,89,118
Trout, Robert, 37,118
Trueblood, Felicity,
150,153-55
Tumulus, 7

Turner, Adolphus,
175
Turner, Larry, 150
Turnipseed, Joseph,
78,79
Turpentine mills, 57
Turtle Suppers, 83
Two Mile Pond, 11
Tyre, Hazel, 175
Tyre, Irving, 175
Tyre, Paul, 175
Tyre, Roy, 175

U.S. 26, 11
U.S. Congress, 10
U.S. Env. Protection
Agency, 169
U.S. Nat. Reg. of
Historic Places,
145,150,154,161
U.S. Territory, 10
Underwood, Cecil,
115
Union soldiers, 16
Union, 13
United Methodist
Church, 34,35,59
United States,
12,34,170
Univ. of Florida,
8,148,156
Univ. of Florida Ar-
chives, 51
Univ. of Florida
Foundation, 148
Univ. of New York,
18

Vaught, A., 155
Vaught, Alfred, 175

Veterans, 2,101,124
Vietnam War Veterans, 175
Virginia, 36
Vitachuco, 11
Vogelbach Pharmacy, 62
Vogelbach, Elmira, 65
Vogelbach, H.A., 86
Vogelbach, Major, 50
Vogelbach, Wm, 84
Von Nostzky, Hans, 11,84,96,99
Von Nostzky, Mrs. Hans, 99
Vurnakes, George, 145

Wakulla Springs, 5
Waldo Canal, 29
Waldo, FL, 14,15,24-28,31,33,36,82,105, 171
Wall, Lawrence, 172
Wallach's Melrose Delight, 51
Walterburg, SC, 153
Walters, Frank, 175
Ward, Martin L., 172
Ward, Sidney, 175
Ware, Jessie, 173
Warren, Fuller, 74
Warren, K., 168
Warren, Pat, 19
Washington, DC, 103
Waters, A.H. 56,91
Watkins, Caroline, 24

Watkins, M., 155
Watkins, Maud, 143,145,153
Watts, Thomas, 175
Waugh, C.V., 87
Webber, Carl, 25,27
Weber, Bertha, 97
Weber, Charles, 97
Weeks, J.C., 175
Weeks, R.B., 172
Welcher, Vickie, 150
West Florida, 10
Western Railroad, 55
Westfield, NJ, 77
Westgaard Family, 57,59
Westgaard Sawmill, 57,58
Westgaard, Ida, 58
Westgaard, Mrs., 58
Westgaard. Gertrude, 58
Weston, Isaac, 30,172
Wheeler, Linda, 167
Whitehead, E.J., 96, 99
Whitehead, Mr., 82
Whitehead, Mrs. E.J., 99
Whiterock bass, 158
Whiting, Pamela, 137
Whitney, Andrew 175
Whitney, Ernest, 106,142
Whitney, Mr., 126

Whitney's Garage, 119
Wiles, Noah, 172
Williams, E., 153,155
Williams, Edna, 167
Wiper fish, 158
Wolf, John., 86
Wolfe Family, 40
Wolfe, Emily, 40
Wolfe, John, 40
Wolfe, Lynol, 40
Woodmen of the World, 83
Works Progress Admin., 111
World War I, 66,101, 112
World War II, 119, 124
Wright, Melvin, 167
Wyman, Mrs., 118
Wyman, Windsor, 105
Wynwood Street, 54

Yarbrough, Elmo, 175
Yazoo City, MS, 36
Yearwood, W., 84
Yerkes, Fred, 111
Yesterday in Florida, 8,36,38,40,41,47,49, 50,58,59,67,89,104, 109,118
Yulee Railroad Days, 164
Yulee, David, 14,164